HEARTQUAKE

Lilya Wagner

Pacific Press Publishing Association
Mountain View, California
Oshawa, Ontario

Designed by Paul B. Ricchiuti
Cover illustration by Sue Rother

Copyright © 1983 by
Pacific Press Publishing Association
Printed in United States of America

Library of Congress Cataloging in Publication Data

Wagner, Lilya, 1940-
  Heartquake.

  (Daybreak)
  1. Wada, Toshimasa, 1945-   . 2. Seventh-day Adventists—Japan—Biography. 3. Seventh-day Adventists—United States Biography. 4. Converts, Seventh-day Adventist—Biography. I. Title.
BX6193.W23W33   1983   248.2'44'0924 [B]   82-18771
ISBN 0-8163-0510-2

Chapter One

Diving low, the screeching bombers released destructive cargoes stashed in their bellies. Bombs plummeted to the earth, sending deadly shockwaves through the tranquil Japanese countryside. Behind the home-bound planes, smoke, dust, and fire rose from bombed-out factories, homes, and schools.

Yoko, the midwife, peered through the black curtains. She had heard the explosions and on tiptoe had scurried to the window. Now she glanced down from the second-story height and saw people clustered on the street corners and in front of the house. Excitedly they pointed toward the south, toward Tokyo. Yoko checked the window, closed tightly to subdue the noises of war, and pulled the curtains together to shut out the eerie red glow. Right now she couldn't take time to find out what the town of Aioi Mura was talking about.

Soon the silence of the room was broken by a wail. Yoko smiled as she cleaned the baby and took it to the tired mother. "Look," Yoko whispered. "The Wada family now boasts a fine son!"

Mamiko cradled the baby. "A son," she repeated. A crash in the distance punctuated her statement, and the windows rattled. Mamiko lay back wearily. "It's

1945," she spoke softly. "The year has just begun. And American planes bomb us more every day. Japan needs good leaders. Yes, when Kenji comes back from fighting, we will pick just the name. This boy will become great!"

Yoko nodded and took the baby from its mother. War had made her work much harder, she reflected, with all the anxious mothers, the tense atmosphere, and the bombing creeping north from Tokyo. But she never could help smiling when she held a healthy baby. At those times the war faded into muted sounds in the distance.

Several weeks later Mamiko and Kenji sat at the low table in the main room. "We need to choose a very strong name," Kenji said, looking at the Japanese characters before him and picking up a pen. "Someday my son will become a leader in Japan!"

Mamiko stared at the paper on the table. "Yes," she murmured, already intent on examining the meaningful symbols in front of her.

In the next room the baby cried. Mamiko started to get up, but Kenji placed a detaining hand on her arm. "This is important. Let Mother take care of him." Together they chose characters, drew them in combinations, discarded some, selected others, all the time trying to draw special meaning from the symbols.

Finally they looked at each other, satisfied. "Look. We've got it now," Kenji spoke. "See. Toshi is first. That means he is quick or intelligent. Then Masa. That means he will be a general or leader. Look how the strokes all match evenly and are balanced!" He turned and called, "Mother, come. We have named the mayor's great-grandson!"

A short figure scurried in. She cuddled the child and looked over her son's shoulder. A low exclamation escaped her lips. "That's a fine name!" She straightened and looked at her son and daughter-in-law. "Tomorrow we will let the relatives know. We must celebrate!" She turned and repeated to no one in particular as she left the room, "Yes, a fine name!"

Toshimasa grew amid comfort and security, unaware of the turmoil that swirled around him. Japan lay in defeat. Just six months after his birth, the shock of Hiroshima and Nagasaki had reverberated around the world. Japan's cities, economy, and morale lay in ruins. Added to that were the vast social changes brought about by the occupation forces. Only gradually did the trauma of war begin to fade. But Toshimasa knew nothing of this. Neither did he experience hunger. Had he been older, he might have realized how many people in Aioi Mura worried about their next meal. Instead, he awoke every morning to a Hershey's chocolate bar on his pillow. He didn't miss the parents who left it there, either. His grandmother dressed him, fed him, supplied him with toys, proudly showed him off to friends and neighbors, and hugged him a lot as she murmured, "Toshimasa, you are special."

Sometimes Toshimasa's parents returned home before he went to sleep. Then he lay awake and listened to their voices.

"No, we didn't get caught," he heard his father say one night. Toshi crept out of bed and sat on the top step, listening.

"We got another lead on a farmer who is willing to exchange some more rice and potatoes for father's beautiful silk garments," Mamiko's voice drifted upstairs. "Then we can sell the food for more money. There are so many people willing to buy on the black market! But I do get nervous when we're around the national police." Mamiko's voice died away.

"Ah, don't be foolish." Kenji, Toshi's father, strolled into the living room, a cup of sake in his hand. He turned to Grandmother. "Don't look so worried! We don't go past the checkpoints. We cut through the woods and fields and catch the train at secluded stops. Besides, the officials are less suspicious when they see a well-dressed couple together. Looks innocent." He threw back his head and tossed off the drink.

For a few minutes no one said anything. Toshi's five-year-old mind couldn't grasp the meaning of what he heard, and he almost went back to bed. But because he seldom saw his parents, he felt a little curious about them, and now he wanted to watch and listen to them.

Kenji broke the silence. "We're just lucky that we live in a town famous for its silk industry. This way we have something to trade for food—and a way to make a little money! Everyone likes pretty clothes. Besides," Kenji looked at Mamiko, "we're lucky that your father and brother have their own factory. Of the hundreds of little silk factories in this town, theirs must be one of the best."

"Yes," Mamiko answered, "it's a great way to make quick money and get food for ourselves besides. Let me have your money. I'll put it away." Toshi heard the rustle of her dress as she rose from her seat and moved out of the room.

"Yes, put it away," Kenji's voice boomed. "When our neighbors and friends in Aioi Mura start to get back on their feet, we'll be rich."

Toshimasa tiptoed back to bed, laid his head on the pillow, and, while voices faded into the distance, he drifted to sleep.

Toshimasa may have wondered about his parents, but only with passing, childish interest. When he awoke each morning, grandmother always fussed over him. She dressed Toshi in his best outfits and took him on walks in Aioi Mura. Other times Toshi followed her around and sang to her as she worked. Toshi often sang. He listened to popular tunes on the radio and mimicked them closely. One day Grandmother suddenly stopped ironing, looked at Toshi as if she had never really heard him sing before, and sat down. "My, you really sound nice!" She took him by the shoulders and smiled. Toshi grinned back. Grandmother had an idea. "Toshi, tomorrow let's go to some of the silk factories when they have their breaks, and you can sing for them! And I can tell them you are my grandson!"

The next day Grandmother dressed in her best traditional kimono and patted her neatly done hair. Then she took her five-year-old grandson by the hand, and they walked down the street to the nearest silk factory. The eight employees looked up from their tea break and stared as Grandmother pulled up a little stool, helped Toshi stand on it, solemnly introduced him, then said, "OK, Toshi. Now sing!"

Toshi sang. As he did this day after day, he began to dream that when he grew up he might be popular and famous like those people who made music on the radio. A show-biz singer! He smiled, bowed, and sang. When people offered him money, he graciously accepted it, then turned it over to his proud grandmother.

By the time Toshimasa entered first grade, his parents had stopped their smuggling. They felt they no longer needed to deal in black-market trade to get enough food for their family. Mamiko had tucked away the extra money they had made by trading silk for food to sell, and both she and Kenji decided to supplement these savings by more respectable means fitting to their position in society. Mamiko opened a small store and sold candies and sweets, while Kenji worked at the American air force base. At the end of each week, Mamiko took their surplus earnings and invested them. With growing satisfaction she watched the amount of money increase. Her family lacked nothing, and yet she could save for the future.

Toshimasa had always received the best of everything, but, in first grade he discovered, like most other Japanese children, that he also had to produce the best. At the end of the first semester when he left his first-grade room, he skipped home, raced up the stairs, and greeted his mother. "Look!" Toshi placed something in her lap. "My teacher said I should give this to you."

Mamiko opened the small brown folder. "Your report card," she said. "Why, Toshi!" A frown creased her smooth forehead. "How could you do so poorly! You have only B's and C's! No A's! Father, look!"

Kenji came over and grabbed the folder from her hand. He gave it a quick glance, then scowled at Toshi. Toshi shrank back. He had never met with Father's disapproval before. What had he done wrong?

"Toshi, this is a disgrace!" Kenji stormed. "You—you—" he spluttered in his anger. "You will be severely punished! You can no longer play after school. You will study until you receive all A's."

Toshi struggled to keep tears from his eyes. Never had his father stormed at him like this. He hung his head and slunk out of the room.

Day after day Toshimasa had to study. His parents reminded him that he was intelligent, that he was to be a leader, and that he must excel both mentally and physically. Soon he didn't want to come home after school anymore. He shuffled down the dirt streets of Aioi Mura and lingered to watch corner-lot baseball games, but he didn't dare stay late. At home he slumped over his books; once in a while he stared out the window and rubbed the callus that had formed on his finger.

The end of the second semester came. This time Toshi realized what the little brown folder meant. It was a report card, and now he understood that report cards had a great deal to do with how grown-ups treated him. All during the semester his parents had kept in touch with his teacher and had inspected his work to see if he had done it neatly and correctly.

Shyly he placed the little folder in his mother's lap. "Hmm," she mused "Better this time, Toshi." She rewarded him with a small smile. "Look, Father. Mostly A's and B's."

Kenji barely looked over the folder. "Not good enough," he grumbled. "Toshi must get all A's! Toshi is lazy; he doesn't work hard enough."

Toshi began to experience new feelings. Grandmother still loved him, hovered over him, and praised him, but he yearned for approval of his parents. His grandmother hugged him, but the only physical contact he had with his parents were the punishments. A tightness grew inside that Toshi couldn't explain.

On Sundays Mother sometimes glanced out of the window and said, "Let's go out of the town and paint today. Toshi needs to learn how to draw the fields and streams in perspective, and how to keep his mountains from looking flat. Come, I'll pack a lunch!"

The family headed for the nearby countryside and sat in the peacefulness while the parents sketched and painted. "Look, Toshi," Kenji pointed to the mass of watercolors. "Here's how you mix these two colors to get a blue just right for those mountains."

Mamiko leaned over to look. "Yes, Toshi. Watch carefully how I draw that tree," she said, pointing.

"You must learn to be the finest artist possible!" She smiled happily, but as he bent over his sketching pad Toshi felt his stomach tighten.

When Toshi finished second grade he already knew that he must work hard to keep up his grades. And now his parents urged him to excel in sports just as he had in his classwork. They coached him as he joined them and others on the dirt streets in a game of dodge ball. He participated in the twice-a-year Sports Day at school, but he couldn't run very fast and often missed the ball. "You have duck feet," his parents said. "Why can't you run faster?"

"Perhaps he can do better at judo or kendo than at baseball or track," Kenji suggested after another sports event at school.

"Yes." Mamiko looked thoughtful. "Maybe kendo is the right sport, because he will have to defend himself."

So Toshi began classes in one of the traditional sports of Japan. After some sessions with the bamboo fencing stick, he began to wear the protective gear. Toshi slumped under the weight of the final piece, the headgear. When his teacher turned to pay attention to another student, Toshi ran. He didn't like to practice kendo because the students were taught to hit hard, and he didn't like to hurt anyone. He took a few steps, stumbled, and fell. The heavy headgear had actually toppled him over. He lay there, ashamed, until he regained his breath, then quietly stole back to join the group.

As Toshi moved on to the fourth grade, he frequently felt the familiar tension build inside. Though he tried hard, his parents never seemed satisfied. Maybe he could please them by doing well at the Buddhist temple school where they had enrolled him. He liked calligraphy; his hand curved around the brush, and he watched the letters take shape. Even the classes in abacus were interesting. They seemed useful, and required no running, jumping, or dodging skill.

Sometimes he watched the saffron-robed monks during their worship ritual at the temple and wondered at what they were doing. At home he participated in the morning ceremony of offering food at breakfast time at the altar of Buddha. He listened as one of his parents asked for the god's blessing. Sometimes he joined his grandmother as she prayed to the several ancestral spirits represented on the Shinto shrine, but since these gods seemed so remote he did this mostly to be near her.

One night Toshimasa sat down between his two sisters at the supper table. His mother glanced toward the door before she sat down. "Where's Father?" she asked. "He isn't usually absent when our mealtime comes."

A crash at the door interrupted her. Father burst in, eyes bloodshot, face red, and yelled, "We've lost it! Those fools! We've lost it all!"

Chapter Two

Toshimasa sat frozen in his seat. Mother scurried from the table and tried to calm Father. "What have we lost? Tell me! tell me!" She tried to hold him as he stormed around the room. "What's wrong?"

Toshimasa and his sisters slumped down. They had often watched their father lose his temper, but never in such a rage. Toshi felt his stomach tighten; he looked at his grandmother for reassurance. She didn't look back. Instead she stared intently at her son.

"We're bankrupt!" Father screamed. "We've lost everything!" He sank down on the nearest chair and put his head in his hands.

Mother stared and seemed to struggle for words.

Toshimasa listened with horror as his father continued to rant.

"More than $100,000!" he moaned. He looked at mother. "I didn't know you had saved so much!"

Finally mother seemed to have found her voice. "It's all gone?" she breathed. "All the money I've saved?"

Toshimasa remembered how his mother would carefully count the money that came in every month. He had watched as she put some away—for their living expenses, he presumed. Then she put the rest in a small brown cloth bag. Sometimes he accompanied her to the investment company where she deposited the money. He remembered the warm greetings from the manager, a family friend.

Father's voice jarred him back to the present. "And because Aki is a friend of ours, there's nothing we can do," he yelled. "We can't even trust our friends! We can't do anything to get our money back. He's bankrupt! Bankrupt!" Father again covered his face with his hands.

Mother just stood in the middle of the room. The truth began to sink in, and Toshimasa watched her anxiously. What would she do now?

The next day, before Toshimasa even got out of bed, a knock resounded through the house. Mother went to the door. Her face, tense from the ordeal of the night before, blanched when she saw two policemen standing on the steps. "What do you wish?" she faltered.

"We need to search your home," one policeman stated politely. He made a move to block the door, even though Mother hadn't stirred. "No one is to leave the house."

"But why?" Mother sounded even more frightened.

In a low, calm voice the policeman answered, "We think your husband may have a gun. He was reported to be very angry. Our informant said he thought your husband might shoot someone."

Mother stared as the police moved into the house. They commanded the family not to touch anything. Toshimasa sat silently and watched the police search everything—they pulled out drawers, looked under beds, examined the closets, looked in the kitchen cupboards.

Father had sobered up by now, and he kept trying to tell the police, "Look, all I had with me was this chisel.

I carve wood. I am a carpenter. I don't have a gun," he kept insisting.

After the search turned up nothing, the police had to admit that perhaps the witness *had* only seen a chisel and had mistaken it for a gun. With one more dubious glance over their shoulders, the men left.

But father's rage did not. He began to drink more heavily, and when he came home at night he acted like a madman. "Woman!" he roared at his wife, "why isn't my supper ready!" Mother tried to reason with him, to tell him that she never knew when to expect him. But her words only made him angrier. He began beating her. Mother tried to defend herself or run away, but frequently he overpowered her.

Usually Toshimasa and his sisters were asleep by the time Father came home, but they often woke up and lay quietly, fearful because sometimes he stalked into their rooms and ripped off the quilts, dragged them out of bed, and beat them also.

One night Toshimasa woke up to the yelling and screaming in the living room. He jumped from his bed, rushed to the door, peered through the crack, and watched Father yank Mother around the room. His heart pounded, and he started to run to help her. Then he saw Grandmother run from her bedroom and confront Father. "Don't you hit her!" she commanded and shielded Mother with her tiny body. Toshimasa stared at the sight. The woman glared at her son, who seemed to shrink within himself. Finally he just turned away.

Toshimasa took a deep breath. He only then realized how scared he was watching that fight.

Father now changed jobs and began to work again as a carpenter. Toshimasa admired his skill. Because his father did such exceptional work, he didn't lack business. But Toshi dreaded each new job his father got. Before a house was completed a big celebration took place. The family, friends, and workers would gather around the new home. The festivities always included plenty of alcoholic drink. Toshimasa always hid in the shadows. He knew that each time they celebrated, a fight followed. He shielded his face with his hands, and through the cracks between his fingers he watched Father become the center of the melee.

Toshimasa worried about his mother. He was old enough to realize how hard she worked all day, but now her work increased. He began getting up at 5:30 in the morning. "Mother," he said as he gently pushed her aside, "let me make the fire for you." Mother's tired expression took on a tender character as she turned to fill the pot with rice and water.

Toshimasa also packed a lunch for himself each morning. He placed little clumps of rice in seaweed and wrapped a newspaper around them to keep them warm.

"You're getting quite good at cooking, son," Mother often said.

Toshimasa smiled. He enjoyed the cooking classes at school. As he and his friends got older, they learned how to help out more at home, and the classes prepared them for these chores.

Mother fed the family at 6:30 in the morning, just before she left for work. Frequently she also handwashed laundry before breakfast. Toshimasa would affix two buckets of soapy laundry on his bicycle and carefully wind his way through the streets filled with people also on bicycles. The little road out of the village turned to a narrow path that cut through rice fields. At the river Toshi rinsed the laundry, then hurried back so that he wouldn't be late for school and

Mother would be on time for her job at her father's silk factory. "How I wish I had a motorcycle like Grandfather," Toshi often thought. "Then I could do this fast. But he has the only motorcycle in town!"

In the evenings Mother returned home exhausted by her tedious work and her worry about Father, her family, and money. She seemed to have only enough energy to prepare a simple meal of rice, vegetables, and fish. Some evenings the family sat down without Father. On nights like these Mother would say to Toshimasa, "Oh, it's eight o'clock already. Father should be home, but he isn't. Toshimasa, you will probably find him at Sakura. Please try to bring him home before he spends all the money he was paid today."

Toshimasa hated such errands. He knew how drunk his father could be, and he dreaded confronting him in a gambling hall. He usually found Father at one of the drab, shabby gambling places. He approached timidly. "Father, it's time to go home."

Father remained motionless, his eyes glued to the pachinko machine.

"Get out of my way, boy," he growled.

Toshimasa watched. "Please Father," he pleaded. "Let's go home."

Father didn't answer. Finally Toshimasa sneaked under the machine and grabbed the gambling balls. Quickly he stood up, hiding the balls behind his back. Father scowled. "All the balls—gone already? I lost!"

Toshimasa nodded. He knew that now they could go home, but at a price. On the way home Father grumbled, "I lost. It's your fault." He turned and cuffed Toshimasa on the side of the face.

On another of these almost nightly errands Toshimasa took a detour. He didn't head for Sakura or any of the other gambling halls in the village. Instead he walked toward the railroad tracks and started following them. He walked a while, his mind stirring with thoughts. He felt so alone, so sad. Life had changed so much. With all the newer family troubles, the pressure he had known before seemed less serious. He couldn't even go to Grandmother for comfort, because now she worked to help Mother support the family. He looked at the patched elbows of his school uniform. Yes, things had changed. Mother and Grandmother struggled to feed the family, and he missed the companionship he had had with his grandmother. She now went from silk factory to silk factory, connecting threads on the machines. He knew what tedious work that could be—the thread had to come through tiny holes, and three hundred threads had to be tied to the side of the machine. Then the weaving could begin.

He hated the sadness on his mother's face. She had always been rather serious, but this new sadness frightened him. One evening, ready to burst into the kitchen, he paused suddenly by the doorway. His mother was standing still, staring out of the window. He watched her fearfully, because she usually was always bustling about. Finally he heard her mutter, "I must leave him! But I can't!" She wrapped her arms around herself. "I can't! My family would be disgraced. I can't leave him." Deeply worried Toshimasa left quietly. He knew of a few times when his mother had run from his father's beatings to her own mother and father, but she always returned.

After walking for a time along the tracks, he sat down on them and waited, wondering what it would be like if he just lay down and let a train run him over.

Finally he got up. Mother expected him to find Father and bring him home. He promised himself that he would return to the tracks and think about suicide some more. Did he have any other way out?

By the time Toshimasa reached the sixth grade he regularly helped his family by working at any jobs possible. That summer Grandmother had an idea. "Toshimasa, the workers in the factories take several breaks in the day," she said.

Toshimasa nodded. He knew in the winter they broke at ten o'clock for tea break; but in the summer they preferred ice-crush drinks.

"You can deliver the ice-crush to them," Grandmother continued. "I'll get the orders, and when we know who wants what, you can take it out to them."

Toshimasa piled the little glasses filled with the colorful ice-crush—made with strawberry, sweet bean, honey orange, or other kind of flavor—into the basket on his bicycle. He balanced the load of ten to twenty little glasses with one hand and pedaled as fast as he could. Sometimes he met with disappointment. "The ice is half melted," the foreman said as he stared at the miserable sight of half-full glasses. "We're not going to pay you the full amount." Toshimasa fought back the tears. Next time he'd have to pedal faster.

Grandmother suggested, "Why don't you pile it up higher and figure how far you have to go? Then it won't be quite so melted by the time you get there." That worked. Toshimasa crushed and delivered ice all summer. He put his earnings into a savings account and watched the amount grow—just like his mother had watched hers.

When Toshimasa finished sixth grade that year his family came to his graduation. The auditorium looked splendid with all the decorations, and the music and speeches were grand. At the end of the ceremony the time came for awards. Toshimasa sat with his class members and watched as some were called to the front. Suddenly he heard his name, "Toshimasa Wada." He jumped up and headed for the platform, listening to what the principal had to say. "Toshimasa receives a special award because he has been very industrious. A committee has selected his name, and we are pleased to give him this honor." Toshimasa walked to the platform in a daze. He could barely muster up a grin as he received the award and returned to his classmates.

After the ceremony his parents met him and congratulated him. Although he felt a quiet pleasure that he had been able to please them, he still felt that they didn't approve of his lack of achievement in some areas. True, he had won many awards for his art by now, but his parents expected him to excel in other areas. He still avoided the neighborhood boys, most of whom were older than he and enjoyed war games. They made swords from branches and fought each other with a vengeance. Toshimasa stood on the sidelines when these games started. He disliked this kind of violence, and when someone would get hurt and bleed, he would turn and flee down the alley. Neither did he like baseball, a game that had become very popular. "You're acting like a girl," his parents would say.

But now, at his sixth-grade graduation, he had been honored for doing something worthwhile. Father said, "Keep working hard." He looked pleased as he gave Toshimasa a rare pat on the back. "You might become a banker yet. And bankers make a lot of money," he added thoughtfully.

Mother spoke up. "Yes, now that you are learning calligraphy and the abacus, you will be skilled to go into business."

Toshimasa's smile faded. His stomach tightened into

a knot again, and he followed his parents out of the school, his eyes on the toes of his shoes.

He continued to go to the Buddhist temple in the evenings. There he could work up to the third degree in abacus training, the minimum required for being a banker. The temple didn't charge any tuition unless the student received private tutoring.

Although Toshimasa liked the classes, he rarely attended a Buddhist service. The morning worship at 3:30 drew few people, but at home the family continued the ritual prayers in front of the Buddhist and Shinto shrines. Toshimasa knelt before the beautifully made cabinet bearing his ancestors' names on a golden plaque. At other times he worshiped by the Shinto altar, praying to one of the several gods that he believed controlled his world.

One day the Buddhist priest honored him with a special request. "Toshimasa," he said, "you have been attending our classes regularly, and you have worked hard. Your behavior has been excellent. Will you now assist in the services?"

Toshimasa bowed his head. He felt special. Not many children his age were selected for this kind of service. He felt rewarded for sticking to his work in the classes even though many of his peers had dropped out. After all, the classes called for self-discipline and concentration. "Yes," he replied with a humble bow, "I will be honored."

Each week he sat in the service. He tried to understand what the priest talked about, but much of it escaped him. He knew that when the priest hit the gong he should bow his head, but he didn't know why. He sat and listened to the gong, to the chanting priest, and to the rhythm of the temple blocks. The beat increased in speed and pitch, and each phrase climaxed in a sounding of the gong. Again he bowed. Incense swirled around his head.

Only once in a while did Toshimasa understand the priest. He should be trying to better himself. Buddha is watching him. Buddha will drop a fine string, like that of a spider web. He should grab it and start climbing to Buddha with his own power. Buddha would not pull him up.

The priest illustrated with a story. "Once there was a man who found this special string and came up half way. He looked up at Buddha and said, 'Well, I'm moving up,' when he heard a noise behind him. He looked down and saw many men climbing up the same string after him. Alarmed he screamed, 'Hey, fellows, get down. I'm going up there; you guys get down. The string's going to break.'

"Buddha, watching, said, 'Well, he hasn't learned yet.' Then he dropped the whole string, and all the men fell."

Toshimasa pondered this. "I must not be selfish," he said to himself. "Buddha will judge how good a life I lead. I can't condemn and criticize other people. I want to be good," he decided.

In junior high school the pressure to achieve increased. Now Toshimasa had to prepare for entrance into a high school. Each month his class was tested, and ratings were publicly announced. If he kept a certain position in this ranking, he could go to high school. Toshimasa feared the keen competition. He knew that if he wanted to work in a particular job or for a certain company, he had to attend the right schools, and that meant getting a good rating.

So Toshimasa pushed himself to get even better grades. He also determined to improve at sports. Although he had learned baseball, he still couldn't hit the ball well. "Maybe I can try ping-pong," he thought. He joined the club. During the first year he had to practice two hours every day, but only after the upperclassmen had finished. That meant many times he and his teammates had to play in the dark. "That's a challenge," the coach would say. He blindfolded the students, and they had to stand and listen to the ball strike, then judge its speed and direction. Toshimasa developed such a sensitivity that after a while he could play quite well in the dark. He entered the city tournament. By the time he got to high school he achieved a position among the top ten in the city.

At the beginning of Toshimasa's seventh-grade year the talk around the school buzzed with news about a new music teacher. "Have you seen him?" the students whispered to each other. "He isn't mean like the last teacher, and he isn't old!" Toshimasa could hardly wait to get to music class. Already he played the accordion that he found at home and had spent some of his precious money on a harmonica.

In class the teacher displayed several instruments. "Now, I will let you try these," he told the students. Toshimasa sat on the edge of his seat, impatiently waiting for his turn.

Finally the teacher brought him a flute. "Here," he said. "This is how you blow it." And the magical note floated through the room.

Toshimasa tried. His teacher looked at him in surprise. "That's well done!" he praised Toshimasa.

From then on Toshimasa came to school early, sometimes even at six o'clock in the morning. He let himself into the dark band room and practiced the flute until eight o'clock. "I can hardly believe your progress," his teacher said. "We ought to get you your own flute."

That night Toshimasa approached his parents. He hung his head and mumbled, "I want to have a flute. My teacher thinks I should have one."

His parents stared at him in surprise. An awkward pause followed. Then his father spoke angrily, "Of course not! That is not the profession we want you to pursue. Unthinkable!"

Toshimasa could think of nothing else to say. He left the room, but disappointment so filled him that he wanted to lie on his bed and cry.

When his teacher heard about this he said, "I'll go to your home and talk to your parents."

Toshimasa didn't think that would help, but he agreed to the plan. His teacher spoke to Toshimasa's parents. "Your son is extraordinarily talented in music," he explained. "If you can't buy him an instrument, then will you let me buy one for him? He must be able to practice and to play."

The parents glared at the teacher. A stony silence filled the room. Finally they answered, almost in unison, "No!" His mother continued, "That is not the profession we have in mind for Toshimasa. He must give up this foolish ambition. He must become a leader, a famous person."

Defeated, Toshimasa decided, "Well, if I can't study it like I want to, at least I'll have fun with music." He found it too painful to continue on the flute, so he picked up the trumpet. It was great, blasting out those notes. Then he heard a visiting band that came to town, the United States Air Force Band. "This is too good to be true," he said to himself. He paid special attention to the trumpeters. Back at school, early in the mornings in the dark band room, he imitated what he had heard.

He began to play in concerts, and each time invited

his family. Grudgingly, they began to appreciate this achievement. Mother was mildly enthusiastic after a few concerts. "You're doing nicely." She smiled at him. Father grunted, but Toshimasa could tell by the tone that he approved. They wanted Toshimasa to excel, and this was one way of doing it.

Grandmother, however, was thrilled. She took Toshimasa aside one day and confided, "Look, Grandson. I have saved this money from my work in the silk factories plus my pension. I want you to go to Tokyo and buy yourself a trumpet."

Toshimasa stared in amazement. What would Father think?

To Toshimasa's surprise, Father didn't object. In fact, he accompanied Toshimasa to Tokyo. Toshimasa looked at the trumpets, carefully and tenderly held each in his hands, then tried it out. Finally he bought a British-made model. Gently he cradled it all the way home. Father looked at him, then said, "Of course, after you finish high school, you'll work for me as a carpenter. And then maybe you will become a banker."

Toshimasa sighed and looked out of the train window as it passed simple brown country houses, green forests, and fields. Would it ever be possible for him to study music, he wondered.

In the ninth grade Toshimasa studied harder than ever. He had to prepare to enter high school, and that looked like a formidable task. When school dismissed at 3:00 p.m. he went first to special preparatory classes for the entrance examinations, and then in the evening to the home of his private tutor. There, until 10 p.m. the tutor helped him in English and mathematics. When he finally got home, he continued to study. How often he had heard that if a person slept more than five hours a night while in high school he would be guaranteed to fail. Well, he might as well get used to that regimentation. His eyes blurred as he tried to focus them on the words, and finally the book slipped from his grasp and he slept.

On the monthly ratings he usually managed to remain among the top three in his class of 209 students. On one dreadful occasion when he slipped below the top three to sixteenth place, his teacher visited his home and told his parents, "Your son has disgraced himself and you. He is in sixteenth place. If he continues in this, he will not be able to attend high school." The teacher's stern gaze shifted to Toshimasa. "You must work harder. Next time your scores must improve."

Finally the time for entrance examinations arrived. Toshimasa wrote for two days, then waited for two tense weeks until the results would be posted.

He tried to appear nonchalant as he walked to the school auditorium, but his heart beat so loudly that it reverberated in his ears, and he thought everyone must surely be hearing it too. He entered the auditorium and looked at the lists on the walls. Around him the talk swirled. "Did you make it? What was your score? Will you go to high school?" He watched the rejoicing, tried not to hear the crying, and looked for the W's. He found the sheet, closed his eyes, breathed hard, and finally found the courage to read his scores. A slow grin spread over his face. He made it! He breathed a long sigh of relief. Now he had something to tell his parents that should make them proud of him! Now he could attend the best high school in the town, the second best in the whole prefecture.

At home Toshimasa waited until the family had gathered for the evening meal, and then he announced as calmly as he could, "I passed the entrance exams. I will be able to go to high school!"

His parents looked up with surprise, then smiled, and all around the table the smiles spread. No one hugged. To hug was considered improper conduct, but they smiled and clapped their hands. "We will invite the relatives to celebrate! This is special," his mother exclaimed.

Toshimasa looked down at his rice bowl. He felt good. Very few of his junior high school classmates would attend high school. Most of them now had to start work. Maybe he would have more chances to strive toward his ambitions, to study music, to do something creative besides becoming a carpenter or banker or army general.

But his parents hadn't given up on the idea. They still determined he would honor his family by becoming a banker. He continued to attend the classes at the Buddhist temple. Now he decided the time had come for him to repay the monks for all the free classes he had received. He approached the priest and said, "I would be happy to tutor others. Many students can't pay, and I can do the tutoring here."

The priest gladly accepted the offer. Toshimasa took up his tutoring duties, and the priest watched him carefully. One day he spoke to Toshimasa privately. "You have done well," he praised Toshimasa. "You have been a good student, and now you are a good tutor. I want you to consider becoming a priest."

Toshimasa looked at the priest and realized he felt no special attachment to the Buddhist religion. Mostly he had attended the temple out of duty, because it was the traditional and proper thing to do and because he could take free classes. But maybe being a priest might be a good idea. Many priests became teachers. They had a guaranteed income because parishioners paid a regular amount as part of their religion. Also being a priest held a certain status and prestige. "I'll think about it," he said.

The priest patted him on the back and turned to go back to the temple. Toshimasa headed home. A priest. What would his parents think?

Toshimasa didn't tell his parents about this new idea, not just yet. If he became a priest, he thought, perhaps he couldn't continue studying music and playing his trumpet. He pondered. Music had become more important in his life. He sang in several choirs and frequently directed the high school band. When the director failed to come to rehearsals, Toshimasa and some of his classmates picked out the music and rehearsed it. The director then appeared for a rehearsal or two before the concert and with a great deal of showmanship led the band. Toshimasa didn't mind. He enjoyed being one of the student conductors. Besides, more often now the director featured him as soloist, and Toshimasa enjoyed that. Each time the applause seemed louder, and his parents began to enjoy the honors heaped on him as much as he did.

During one particular concert Toshimasa played a solo with the band, an arrangement of a popular Japanese tune. The audience went wild. After the concert a huge American with a wide grin, dressed in a strange, brown, flowing garment, came up to Toshimasa. He extended his hand enthusiastically and exclaimed, "That was a beautiful solo! I'd like to get to know you better."

Chapter Three

Toshimasa felt his hand grasped in a strong grip, and he stared up at the jolly, cheerful face. Compared to most Japanese, Toshimasa stood tall at 5′ 10″, but this man dwarfed him. He forced his attention back to what the man was saying. "Why don't you join us? We get together once a week for about two hours and study English together—many young people. You'd enjoy their company, you know." He released Toshimasa's hand. "Oh, yes. We meet at the Catholic church." He gave Toshimasa a companionable clap on the back and left.

Toshimasa realized that if the man had indeed introduced himself, he'd missed it. "Who was that?" He turned to one of the other band members.

"Oh, he's a missionary. From America—a Catholic, a Franciscan, I think."

Now having met him, Toshimasa became more aware of Father Joseph. The Franciscan priest certainly couldn't be missed as he zoomed around the village on his Honda moped. He must have weighed well over 250 pounds, and his hearty laugh could be heard all over the neighborhood. Toshimasa thought he looked like a cartoon character.

Intrigued by the invitation, Toshimasa thought it

might be interesting to improve his high school English abilities. Then he hesitated. He had already been approached by the Buddhist priest, and the invitation to become a priest himself had come as an honor—and a tempting one. He did feel some loyalty to the Buddhist religion, although he had never really examined what that loyalty meant or exactly what he believed. Perhaps he shouldn't start mixing with the people of another religion so unlike his traditional one.

But when Toshimasa discovered that many of his friends in the band and choir attended these classes, as well as the girls from the elite high school in the town, he decided it would be a great chance for some social life. Besides, he did want to improve his English skills—one never knew when they might come in handy.

The first night he went to the Catholic church he lingered in the hall, unsure of where he should go. About two hundred people mingled in the hall and classrooms—people his age, younger students from the junior high, business people. Then Father Joseph spotted him, and his voice boomed through the building. "Toshimasa! Come to this room. I'll meet with these people first." Toshimasa discovered that, in spite of his size, Father Joseph had energy to spare as he went from room to room, instructing the students in English conversation and giving them directions on how to help each other and the younger students.

By the time Toshimasa entered his senior year in high school his urge to study music had become even stronger. He wanted to learn more, to play professionally, to teach. He began to plead with his parents. "Please," he would say, "it is something I feel I must do!"

After many unpleasant arguments they gave in.

Then Toshimasa sadly realized that in obeying his parents and respecting their wishes in the traditional Japanese manner, he had delayed the necessary study and preparation for the college entrance exams. "Well," he thought, "only ten out of three hundred in our class aren't planning to go to college. The rest had to study hard to take the entrance exams. I might as well have fun with my music." So he joined the semiprofessional orchestra in town, continued to perform with his high school band, and sang in several choirs.

But Toshimasa still had to take the college entrance exams, even though he realized he probably couldn't get into the music school at the Gunma University, since they could only accept fifteen students that year. In fact, he didn't think he could get into any music school.

As he sat pencil poised over the paper, he glanced around. What chance did he have? Many of his classmates had been preparing for this since they began high school. Others in the room had completed high schol one, two, even five years before and kept coming back and trying to get a better score. No, he didn't have much of a chance.

After graduation Toshimasa didn't share the excitement and apprehension many of his classmates felt, because he didn't expect to do well on the college entrance exams. When his friends talked about their futures and the schools they intended to attend, Toshimasa often felt left out.

Then the news buzzed around the town. The exam results appeared in the evening paper! Toshimasa didn't hurry home to read the results. He sauntered along the streets, greeted friends, stopped in a bookstore, and finally arrived home. After supper he picked up the paper, turned to the list of scores, and studied them. Finally, he laid the paper down and faced his parents. "I'm ninety-seventh on the list," he informed them. "I'll be graduating in the top third of my class." Father began to speak, but Toshimasa interrupted him. "But I didn't get into music school," he spoke softly. "I scored as number sixteen—they will take only fifteen. If someone decides to go elsewhere or not go to school at all, they might take me." He watched his parents intently. He knew that they always wanted him to rank at the top of anything he tried, to beat the competition. But he also knew they didn't want him to go to college because they had other ideas of how he could become important and famous. He waited.

Father drew a deep breath and then said, "Oh, well. You can work for me now." He turned to leave the room. Just before he got through the door Toshimasa spoke.

"Father," his tone remained soft, but his father stopped suddenly. "Father, if I get accepted, will you suppport me?"

Father didn't turn around, but mumbled, "It's too much money; we can't afford it." Then he went through the door. Toshimasa stood still, looking after him. He now knew that it didn't matter whether he got in or not. He wouldn't have the money. Even though the government university music department didn't cost much, his parents wouldn't give him the money. He sighed deeply and left the house. Maybe something else would work out—someday.

A few weeks after graduation Toshimasa went to work for a textile company. Often as he shifted the papers on the desk and headed for the typewriter he yawned, fighting back boredom. Most of his time he spent filling out business papers in English. Now he had more of a reason to continue his study of English. Besides, Father Joseph had said to him the last time they met, "You're doing so well. Why don't you come to get some private tutoring? We'll study the catechism in English."

Toshimasa answered, "Well, great." He didn't know what a catechism was, but he couldn't see any harm in studying it since it meant learning English better and faster. And he liked Father Joseph. Private tutoring meant he would get to know the genial man better. He had already noticed Father Joseph's generous spirit. He knew little about the Franciscan order and St. Francis, its founder, but he had learned enough to realize that Father Joseph certainly represented well the founder's ideals of self-denial, love, and generosity toward others. Father Joseph attended every special event, whether a fair at the elementary school or a high school athletic festival. He shook hands with everyone and spread his good will throughout the town. Toshimasa couldn't help comparing him to the Buddhist priest who had also befriended him. He had noticed that the Buddhist priest often argued with his wife and at times beat her; he never seemed cheerful and appeared to be very money-hungry. Whenever he did something for someone, even something as simple as saying an extra prayer for a beloved ancestor, he demanded quite a bit of money.

Father Joseph, on the other hand, acted just the opposite. He always threw open the door of the rectory and boomed, "Oh, come in, come in!" and served his company coffee and sweets, especially doughnuts. People liked to be around him. And Toshimasa also had observed his shabby clothing. His robe, torn in one corner, looked dusty and worn. When he took his shoes off, Toshimasa spotted a hole in the bottom. He began to realize that Father Joseph didn't spend much on himself but always gave it away. Of course he got a small allowance, but by the end of the first week of the month, it had been spent on people other than himself.

Toshimasa admired this kind of behavior. He had often wondered why his parents held onto their money so tightly. What good had it done them? he mused. They had lost it after all. Of course, his grandmother was generous, and she also shared her love without restraint. With regret Toshimasa finally admitted to himself, "But my parents didn't share much of anything—either love or money." He sighed. He remembered the times he sat by the railroad tracks and watched the trains whiz by. He had wondered how it would feel if he threw himself in front of those wheels. He shook off the memory and went to keep his appointment with Father Joseph.

"OK, son." Father Joseph settled his bulk down in a comfortable chair. "Let's start." First he tried to read the catechism from a Japanese book written in Roman characters, but Toshimasa couldn't understand what the Father wanted to say. His pronunciation sounded terrible.

Then Toshimasa tried to ask a question, but Father Joseph's Japanese just wasn't adequate to carry on a deep discussion, and Toshimasa's English remained elementary. "Ah, well," Father Joseph said as he laid the book down, "we'll try again."

Each week they met and plodded through the catechism. When they finished it, they started on it again. While on the third time through, Toshimasa met Father Joseph's companion, young Father Mark. The younger priest loved sports and invited Toshimasa to go ice skating, a real treat since he had never done this before. Then, to repay the favor, Toshimasa offered to help Father Mark clean up the ugly churchyard. While they worked Father Mark turned to Toshimasa and said, "I'm the choirmaster at this church. Since you love music so much, why don't you come and sing with us?"

Tosimasa hesitated, but he never could refuse an offer involving music. "Let me see the music," he requested, and they entered the church.

In a few weeks he sang the Latin words in a strong tenor voice, but had no idea what they meant. He did like being in the choir, and he especially loved hearing Father Mark sing. One Sunday the young priest sang "Ave Maria." Toshimasa leaned forward. Music like that had to be heaven-sent, he thought as he sank back against the hard bench.

One day Father Mark called Toshimasa into his office. "Toshimasa," he began, "I've been transferred."

"Oh, no!" Toshimasa replied.

Father Mark looked Toshimasa straight in the eye. "Would you consider taking over the choir? No one else is capable, except maybe the organist, but he needs to play the organ."

Toshimasa stammered, "But I don't know the liturgy. I don't know what the words mean, I'm confused about the time to kneel or to bow."

"But I'll help you," Father Mark urged. "It might also help you to study the catechism harder, so you would know what we believe."

All the things that had confused Toshimasa finally began to fall into place. He understood what the words in the music meant and how they fit with the worship service. Father Mark worked with him twice each week, until Toshimasa felt capable of handling the choir.

On Sundays people often came to him after the services and said, "Your choir is beautiful. You must be proud to be such an active member of this church."

"But I'm not a member," Toshimasa protested.

"You're not baptized?" People always seemed surprised at that and then urged him to join such a great church.

Toshimasa thought about this. For almost a year he had been involved with the church. He had abandoned the idea of becoming a Buddhist priest. But join this church? He was far from sure. He wanted to talk to Father Joseph about it.

"Discuss it with your parents," the Father suggested. "I know you are the oldest in the family and the only son, and you must respect their wishes. See what they will say."

Toshimasa cringed. He didn't think they'd object very much, but he tried to keep away from having any confrontation with his father. He decided to approach his mother first.

That evening he visited his mother in the hospital. She had had surgery only a few days earlier, but he thought that by now she must feel better and he could possibly ask her about joining the Catholic Church.

As they visited Toshimasa finally worked up the courage to say, "Mother, I want to be baptized into the Catholic Church."

She eyed him, paused for a moment, then answered, "It's all right with me." She hesitated. "But you need to ask your father."

Toshimasa waited for a week. He watched his father and tried to spot the right moment when he seemed to be both sober and in a good mood. One evening the time seemed right. "Dad," he blurted out, "I have a really important thing to discuss with you." He explained how he had been going to the Catholic church and how much that had helped his life. "I would like your permission to join," he concluded. "Mother says it's up to you to decide."

Then Toshimasa held his breath, but father only grinned. "It's OK. If it's going to help you be a better person, then it's OK."

A few weeks later Father Joseph met with Toshimasa in the darkened church. In the flickering candlelight, Toshimasa watched as Father Joseph made the preparations. He lighted a smaller candle from the large Easter candle. Then he turned to Toshimasa, poured a little water on Toshimasa's forehead, made the sign of the cross, and put a little salt on his tongue. Then he spoke, "Now you need a new name." He thought for a moment, then his eyes flashed with inspiration. "Francis! We'll name you after our patron saint—because you also are sensitive and kind."

Toshimasa bowed his head, honored that Father Joseph had paid him such a high compliment. Francis, he thought to himself. Nice name. But, I won't use it quite yet. It would be too confusing. I'll put it as my middle name.

Now Toshimasa handled his duties as music director with new enthusiasm. He felt like he belonged, and he wanted to do his best. That Christmas the choir sang especially well, and he felt proud and pleased that the musical portion of the mass had gone so well. Apparently some American visitors in the audience felt the same. After the mass they approached Toshimasa and said, "What a lovely Christmas Eve service! We were pleased to see you as director. Do you remember that we met you about a week ago at the English Club?"

Francis did remember. For some time after the service they chatted, and their friendship grew during the few days the Hills spent in Aioi Mura.

When the family had to leave for Hawaii, where Captain Hill now was stationed, they urged Toshimasa, "You must come to visit us. And come to the United States to study music!"

Toshimasa grinned. "That would be great!" Were all Americans as fine people as these? he wondered.

A few weeks later Toshimasa attended a special band clinic for all the high school bands in his town. Even though he had graduated, his high school band director gave him a special invitation. During the clinic, his teacher said, "Come, I want you to meet an important person." He led Toshimasa to where the visiting musician conducting the clinic stood. Toshimasa's excitement grew. He knew that this man conducted the army band and had composed many pieces for band. Now he felt pleased that his teacher would make the effort to introduce him to this famous musician. They bowed, and his teacher said, "Toshimasa wants to study music, to get into a music school."

The musician studied him thoughtfully and said, "Why don't you join the military band? Then you can still go to school in Tokyo." The more they talked about it, the more excited Toshimasa got.

He decided not to tell his parents about his plans just yet. He winced as he remembered his father sneer, "Toshimasa in the army? Never! He doesn't have the guts for it!" He hadn't intended for Toshimasa to hear this, but Toshimasa had, and he felt hurt.

He visited an army recruiter and volunteered for the service. When the recruiter came to his house to bring some papers for him to sign, his father happened to answer the door. "What?" Toshimasa heard his father's astonished voice. "My son—my son—volunteered for—for the *army*?"

Toshimasa hurried to the door. His father's eyes narrowed. "You? In the army?"

The recruiter told Toshimasa that he would have to take several tests, first the written exam, then some music tests, and finally the physical exam. At that news his father spoke again as he went back into the house. "Oh, well. You won't pass the physical anyway! You can't even play baseball well!"

Toshimasa had already taken the college entrance exams, and he thought the written ones for the army certainly seemed much easier. Then he traveled to Tokyo for the music exam. All day the examiners tested him on sight singing, ear training, theory, history of music, and finally performance. Whew, he thought. I have much to learn.

A few weeks later Toshimasa confronted his father and said, "I have my test results." He paused, waiting to see if his father had any reaction. "I passed." He paused again, then said, "I was the only one from my prefecture who got in the band."

Father grunted. "What about the physical exam? You didn't pass that, did you?"

Toshimasa stood silently for a few minutes. "Yes," he spoke finally. "I passed that too. I'm leaving next week for basic training."

His father's eyes dropped. "Well," he snorted, "you won't last long. You'll be home in a few weeks." Then, more to himself than to Toshimasa, he muttered, "You haven't got the guts."

Chapter Four

Toshimasa sat quietly with his father and mother on the train that rumbled through the Japanese countryside. It moved slowly enough so that each passing scene became part of a panorama rather than a whizzing swirl of colors. He stared out of the window. Although he appreciated his parents' coming to the army base with him, he hoped there wouldn't be any arguments. He still ached inside from his father's words—"You won't make it. You haven't got the guts."

The train whistled a warning and rolled into the outskirts of Tokyo. Toshimasa and his parents boarded the army truck that waited at the railroad station. When the truck stopped after a very bumpy ride, they got out and looked over the scene. The gate framed Toshimasa's new environment, and he didn't know whether he liked it or not. People carried guns, some with alarming nonchalance, and other people screamed loud orders. The colors looked drab and dirty. Toshimasa turned to his father and started to say, "Shall we go in?" when he stopped, startled. In his father's eyes stood large tears, tears ready to spill over and drop on cheeks beginning to wrinkle. Toshimasa wondered whether the sight of the barracks and soldiers had reminded him of his own war experience in the second world war. He didn't know what to say. He had never before seen his father with tears in his eyes.

Wordlessly he started through the gates, his parents following. Toshimasa decided he didn't like what he saw, but he couldn't admit that to his father. He kept silent until they said Good-bye to each other; then he headed for the section of the basic-training camp where his squad would assemble.

He soon heard voices shouting at him too. Along with the other recruits he had to go through the routine procedures. First he stood in line to receive his uniform. When he put it on, he would have laughed—but the stern faces around him silenced him. The uniform hung on him. He went to his sergeant. "Look, sir," he volunteered, "this uniform is too large for me."

He had hardly gotten the words out of his mouth when the man shouted, "Nonsense! And if it is, so what!"

Toshimasa didn't quite see the logic of this pronouncement, but decided he had better keep quiet. The next morning the sergeant summoned him into a room and said, "Sit down here, soldier!" Then he took out some clippers and headed toward Toshimasa's hair. Toshimasa gasped. And he had just spent money getting his hair styled and fixed for his new adventure. The sergeant laid the clippers on his head and cut and cut and cut. Finally all of his hair lay on the floor. He pushed the now bald Toshimasa toward the door and shouted, "Next!" Toshimasa didn't dare look in a mirror.

By noon Toshimasa felt hungry enough to eat two of his grandmother's best meals. He joined the others as they rushed into the camp dining hall where long lines of men served themselves. When he got to the food, he picked up the aluminum pan that would serve as both his dish and his tray. The dish smelled and looked dirty. He sat down with his squad and tasted the dinner. "Ugh!" He grimaced and pushed the tray away from him. "That tastes terrible," he tried to say to his neighbor, but his voice didn't carry over the noise in the hall. He looked at the others around his table and watched them wolf down their food. He sighed and pulled the tray back toward him. He guessed he'd have to get used to it—or starve!

That night, as he got ready for bed, he happened to glance toward the fellow next to him. He watched the soldier pull out his locker and open it. In there Toshimasa spotted a crucifix.

"Hey!" he said. "Are you a Catholic?"

The soldier nodded curtly. He probably expected to be teased about it. Most of the soldiers claimed to be Buddhists or Shintoists, but few expressed concern about religion.

Toshimasa extended his hand. "I'm a Catholic too! It's nice to have you here!"

The soldier grinned and quickly agreed. "You know, I think we're the only two in the squad."

For the first four weeks no one could leave the base. Basic training kept the young soldiers busy, and by the end of the day most gladly sank into their hard bunks for a short night's sleep. But by the second Sunday Toshimasa got up enough courage to approach his sergeant. "Sir," he trembled inwardly as he spoke, "I would like to go to church today. I'm a Catholic. Is this an appropriate thing to ask?"

Toshimasa thought the sergeant would yell at him, but instead the man looked puzzled and said, "I don't know. I'll ask the commanding officer."

A few minutes later the loudspeaker summoned Toshimasa to the phone. Toshimasa heard the voice of his commanding officer on the other end of the line. "What a surprise! To find out that you are a Catholic. I am also!"

Toshimasa started to answer, but the officer went on. "I'll arrange for a special pass for you and your friend and you can go downtown and worship."

Toshimasa thanked him, but the officer interrupted him. "Oh, by the way, after church come by my house and we'll get acquainted."

Toshimasa could hardly believe this kind of thing could happen to him in the army. He got his friend. As they left the barracks Toshimasa's friend pointed to the rows and rows of barracks and said, "Just think! There are 3000 soldiers here, and today, Sunday, only you and I can leave the base. And on top of that we're going to our commanding officer's house."

All of the fifty-three soliders in his squad were musicians, and Toshimasa enjoyed their company as well as their music. As the weeks of basic training went by, Toshimasa's squad grew together in friendship and mutual loyalty. These qualities, Toshimasa felt, helped them work so hard. They received the highest number of points on all the tests, and basking in their commanding officer's praise, they worked even harder.

Three months after the time Toshimasa first entered the gates at the army base, graduation came. His commanding officer called him in. "Toshimasa," he said, "I have a special honor to give to you. You have accumulated the second highest number of points for the entire company. Congratulations!"

In a daze, Toshimasa reached for the extended hand, and then—remembering protocol—saluted. He thought, "And my father said I'd fail!"

The officer continued, "This means a great deal for your future, for promotions. You will receive the first promotion when it comes. And, if you stay in for a longer period of time, you will make much more money!"

With basic training over, the soldiers of Toshimasa's squad got a few days of vacation. Toshimasa went home. Proudly he showed the special certificate to his parents, smiling at their stunned faces. They actually can't believe it, he thought.

"Here, let me have it," Father said. He took it to a neighbor who had been a soldier in World War II.

"Oh, yes. I remember this man," the neighbor exclaimed and pointed to the commander's signature. "I served under him in the war. Toshimasa is greatly honored." And he bowed low.

His parents stared at Toshimasa some more. Finally they clapped their hands together and said, "You're a real soldier! You're a real soldier!"

After the short vacation Toshimasa's squad was transferred to Tokyo, where the army band had its headquarters. Each day Toshimasa attended classes. "Just as if I had gone to the university!" he said to himself. In addition to his classes, Toshimasa practiced four hours every day, took private lessons, and participated in musical groups. Day and night, I'm working on music, he thought. Late at night he would collapse on his bunk and review what he had learned that day. "This certainly is harder than all that physical training we got in the army camp," he muttered.

After the six-month period, those who had continued with the program now graduated. The commanding officer of this particular company called each name. Congratulations and snappy salutes followed. Then came the time for special honors. "I have a special honor to confer on Toshimasa Wada," the commander told the group. "After all the test scores have been compiled, as well as the performance scores and army training, Toshimasa has received the top score!" The assembled group clapped enthusiastically, and Toshimasa beamed. He had succeeded!

Then a Tokyo station contacted Toshimasa. "I'm the producer of the 'To Tell the Truth' program," the voice said. "We would like you to appear on our show."

Toshimasa trembled with excitement as he sat with the two impostors and looked at the moderator and at the panel of famous people, including movie stars. He tried to look nonchalant, but his heart beat fast and his hands felt very sweaty. Outwardly calm, he answered questions about himself—who he was and what he had accomplished. The questioning period ended, and each panelist cast a vote, one for each of the other contestants and two for Francis. Then the moderator requested, "Will the real Toshimasa Wada please stand up?" After the applause, Toshimasa walked to another part of the stage where his band waited. He took the first trumpet position, and they played a popular Japanese tune for the studio audience.

He wondered whether his parents were watching the program, which, after all, was being aired on nationwide TV. He found out soon enough when he got home for another short furlough.

His parents beamed as they greeted him. "Toshimasa, we're so proud of you!"

"Did you see me on television?" Toshimasa wanted to know.

"Yes! Yes!" they exclaimed. "We called the neighbors and relatives, and they're all proud of you too. Tonight we have a big party planned for you—a hero's welcome!"

For the next few days, whenever Toshimasa left home, someone usually accosted him and said, "You must be the one I saw on TV! Can I have your autograph?" Toshimasa couldn't deny that he enjoyed this brief time in the limelight.

After the short vacation at home Toshimasa returned to Tokyo and found out that he had been assigned to the second-best band of Japan. He demurred. "Why can't I be lucky enough to be in the best band?" he asked his commanding officer. He didn't want to complain, but this didn't seem fair.

"Well, it's our policy," the officer answered. "It's our policy to place the top soldier in our second-best band, because they always complain they get the leftovers."

"If it's a policy," Toshimasa sighed, "what can I say?"

Then began the round of concerts until Toshimasa's band had played 150 times that first year. Sometimes they played as many as three concerts a day. Whenever the band happened to play anywhere close to Aioi Mura, Toshimasa received another hero's welcome. His family and friends felt particularly proud of him when he played a solo or in a trumpet trio.

But the routine quickly bored Toshimasa. "I'm tired of playing the same music over and over," he complained to the fellow in the next bunk.

"But remember," his friend reminded him, "if you stay in longer you have a good chance of being an officer in a few years."

"But I don't care about being an officer! Besides, I'm tired of saying 'Yes, sir' and 'No, sir.' It bothers me!"

The shout of "Mail" interrupted the conversation. Toshimasa held the letter he had just received and looked at the return address. Ah! Another letter from his American friends, the Hills.

"Dear Francis," the letter began. Toshimasa smiled. As devout Catholics, the Hills always used the name he received when he joined the church. He himself hadn't quite gotten used to it, since he hadn't wanted to discard his Japanese name. He read on. After news about the family, the letter said, "Why don't you come to Hawaii? Don't you want to study in America?"

Of course, Toshimasa thought. He had considered it even more lately. He wrote back. "Yes, it's my dream to study in the United States, but I need to find a place to stay and some way to finance my studies." Then he added, "But I think I would prefer to study on the East Coast of America." Somewhere Toshimasa had heard that the best and most prestigious schools of music were in that part of the United States. Shouldn't he try for the best? he thought.

The correspondence between Toshimasa and the Hills increased as they tried to work something out for him. The letters served another purpose. Such an exchange of correspondence in English impressed Toshimasa's commanding officers, and they offered him a new kind of position. "Would you consider working as an interpreter for the army?" they asked. "We will send you to a special training school."

Francis declined the offer. Music still interested him the most, and he didn't want to give that up. In spite of his refusal, however, on occasions he did work as an interpreter. He didn't mind, especially when the U.S. Navy Band came to town.

Toshimasa grew increasingly restless. He chafed under the loyalty the army demanded. He wondered whether the kamikaze pilots had dived their planes into the American ships because they believed in the divinity of the emperor or because the army had made life so miserable for them. He had heard rumors of soldiers being tortured during the training sessions back in those earlier days. Maybe some had simply grasped at the opportunity to end it all. He didn't know whether he believed all that. He did know that he could never muster up the kind of loyalty the Japanese army seemed to require.

Life became monotonous. He always played the same music, always felt very tired, always had to look in top shape. It seemed like one round of polishing shoes, hopping into the truck, shivering during the cold, bumpy ride, trying to be pleasant and professional. He was sick of it all.

He thought, "It's time to quit. My term of service is almost up. I want to *really* study."

Then a few months before his discharge Toshimasa received a letter from a friend back home, a member of the English Club.

"Dear Toshi," the letter read. "I had advertised in some American newspapers that I needed a place to stay and work while I learned the laundry business. Some elderly people wrote back and said, 'Yes, you can study here and we will take care of you.' I was just about to leave, when my father got sick and died. I can't go now, as I'm sure you understand. But I feel bad about this old couple, who have written such nice letters to me and say they are looking forward to having me around. Would you go instead?"

Toshimasa laid the letter down. He could hardly believe it! Such luck! Quickly he wrote to the Hills, who had by now moved to Virginia. "Could you please check this out for me? It sounds like the opportunity I have dreamed about."

The round of concerts continued, while Toshimasa chafed under the routine. Finally the answer came from the Hills. He read it eagerly. "Dear Francis, We've discovered that the Speers live only several hundred miles away, so we visited them. The gentleman is a retired naval officer, a famous one. He has written and published textbooks for the navy and naval academy and is an expert on the navy's navigation system. They are one of the richest families in the area. The plan is that you work for them as houseboy and earn money. They will also support your education. You would work a few hours each day and study for the rest of the time. Everyone seems to respect Captain Speer."

Then at the end the Hills added, "Of course, you realize we would enjoy having you with us, but now our children are all in school, and one is in college, and we have neither the room nor the money. Besides, we never know when we might get transferred, with the Vietnam War going on. We think it would be better for a family to take care of you."

"Hurry!" they wrote in closing. "We're looking forward to seeing you in America!"

Chapter Five

"Is this Toshimasa Wada?" asked the voice on the other end of the line. The voice didn't sound familiar.

"Yes," Toshimasa answered, wondering who would be calling long distance.

"This is Captain Tagaki's secretary calling."

Captain Tagaki. Who was he?

"Captain Tagaki received a letter from his friend, Captain Speer, in America," the secretary explained.

Toshimasa did some quick thinking. This call must have to do with his correspondence with the elderly couple in Maryland about his going to the United States to study.

"They are good friends," the secretary continued. "Captain Tagaki was, as I am sure you know, very important in our country's navy and became acquainted with Captain Speer a long time ago."

"What does he do now?" Toshimasa wanted to know.

"He is president of an import and export company and has been doing business with Captain Speer in the United States," the secretary answered. "The captain requested that Captain Tagaki interview you. Can you come on Monday, next week?"

"Yes," Toshimasa stammered. The call caught him

by surprise. He felt awed by this request. What an opportunity! Toshimasa thought.

That evening Toshimasa shared the news with his parents. He knew they would go with him, because whenever a son or daughter received a favor from anyone, the parents would visit that person and take him gifts. And this certainly could be classed as an honor. "Yes, we will accompany you to see Captain Tagaki," his father said. "He is a very important man, and we must plan well, so we will do everything right."

On Monday afternoon Toshimasa and his parents approached a large mansion in Tokyo. At the door, a servant let them in and took them to the beautifully decorated reception room. Toshimasa bowed low as a small man in a traditional kimono approached through the large doors. The man also bowed, but just barely, and said, "I am Captain Tagaki."

He led them to the dining room where his wife waited. Elegantly dressed in a colorful kimono, she greeted them somberly and motioned for Toshimasa and his parents to sit down at the low table.

Toshimasa picked up his bowl of rice and served himself some fish and seaweed. He watched carefully. The formal atmosphere made him very uncomfortable.

He listened to what Captain Tagaki was telling his parents about World War II. "It was very difficult in the war," the captain spoke especially to Toshimasa's father. "I was in Germany. Friends informed me about the war plans. Oh, how I wanted to stop the attack on Pearl Harbor." Toshimasa's attention wandered. He sensed the man was an old-fashioned soldier, a tough one. Where would all this lead?

Then his mind snapped back to the conversation. Captain Tagaki was saying something to him. His stern eyes made Toshimasa sit up and listen. "I believe a person must work hard and sacrifice. There will be hardships, but a person must work hard."

Toshimasa nodded courteously and looked down at his rice bowl. Did the captain try to tell him that he, Toshimasa, wanted an easy way out? Maybe it did seem too easy—just write, ask for a sponsorship, go study in the United States, and become famous.

He listened again. "I had to work very hard," the captain intoned. "I worked long hours, walked many miles to bring home food to feed the children." He droned on, telling Toshimasa and his parents all about his hardships.

Finally the long session ended. As he let them out of the door, Captain Tagaki looked sternly at Toshimasa and commanded, "You will visit me regularly. In fact, you must come work for me, because then I will be able to give an adequate report to my friend, Captain Speer."

On the way home, Toshimasa's parents exclaimed, "What a great oportunity! You can learn much from this famous man." But Toshimasa felt uneasy. He didn't mind working temporarily in the import-export business, but the man made him uncomfortable.

A week later Toshimasa reported for work. "Here. Take this downstairs for me," Captain Tagaki said and handed Toshimasa a folder. When he got back, the captain ordered him, "Go to the dry cleaners and pick up my three suits." In the middle of the day, the captain said, "Go bring me some lunch. I don't wish to leave the office today." By the end of the day Toshimasa sat down wearily and wondered whether he had only imagined it. He had seemed more like an errand boy than a trainee in the import-export business.

The next day Captain Tagaki greeted Toshimasa with another command. "You must wake me up every morning. Since you did not do that today, you can shine my shoes." He motioned toward an extra pair in the office closet. At noon the captain stated, "Now you will massage my back. It gives me difficulty if I sit too long in my office."

At the end of the week Toshimasa stood in line with the other workers, expecting to be paid. He reached the cashier's desk, and the man looked up at him. "What do you want?"

Toshimasa hardly knew what to say. "Isn't there any payment for my work this week?" He distinctly remembered the captain saying, "You must come work for me." He thought that meant he would get paid.

The cashier shrugged. He looked through the pay envelopes, then shook his head. "No," he said, waving Toshimasa off.

He couldn't figure it out. First, the captain expected him to run all his errands and care for him like a personal valet. And all the time he lectured him about humility, about concentration, about the value of manual labor. Toshimasa remembered that one day the captain had suddenly said, "The Speers have had several Japanese work for them." He eyed Toshimasa sternly. "Each has stayed only two or three months."

Now Toshimasa thought about this strange week. He hadn't been introduced to the business at all. He had just done personal work for the captain. Did the captain want to test him? I must be patient, he said to himself. Maybe the captain wants to be sure of me before he lets me have a visa. And I have to measure up to his standards, since he says I will be his representative.

The weeks dragged by. At the end of each week Toshimasa wondered whether he would get paid, but the cashier never had a check for him. Maybe the captain wanted to save the money and give it to him when he left for America. Toshimasa hoped so; this kind of "work and no pay" kept eating at his savings.

One morning the captain had a new idea. "This week you will be going to a religious retreat with me." Toshimasa must have looked surprised and wary, because the captain spoke firmly. "You will not be ready to work in the United States unless you do this."

For an entire week Toshimasa listened to the endless lectures from a group that called itself the "Code of Morality." Some of it made sense, he decided. He could agree with the lectures on humility and service to his fellowman. He didn't mind the ditch digging or setting fence posts. But he had a hard time tolerating Captain Tagaki's constant harrassment. It seemed to him like all he heard was, "Do this! Do that!" What a relief when members of the family or business staff from his company came to visit.

Soon after the religious retreat, Toshimasa received a letter from the Speers in the United States. "When are you coming?" Toshimasa thought the letter sounded somewhat impatient. But he could not be blamed for the delay. He wanted to leave for the United States as soon as he could. "We want you here as soon as possible," the letter went on. "You can go to the Annapolis School of Music. You will be working for us and will be a part-time student." That sounded fair. He didn't expect this couple to support him completely. But he needed a visa to get to America. He wondered briefly about the school of music. Privately he'd hoped to attend the Peabody Conservatory in Baltimore, but maybe Annapolis ranked just as high. Surely people of the caliber of the Speers wouldn't promote anything but the best.

Toshimasa waited for an appropriate moment the next day and timidly requested, "Will you be able to give me a visa this week so that I can leave for the United States?"

The captain roared angrily, "No! You can't go yet! You can't go until I say!"

Toshimasa couldn't argue, because, after all, the Speers had requested Captain Tagaki's opinion. It all seemed up to him now.

Some weeks later, when Captain Tagaki dropped Toshimasa at the train station so that he could spend a weekend at home, Toshimasa had made up his mind.

"I'm not going back," he told Father Joseph. "I don't understand just what's going on," he confided. He explained all the insignificant personal work he had to do for the captain, the lack of payment, the refusal to make it possible for him to get a visa, and the constant lectures from the "Code of Morality."

"Hey," Father Joseph boomed. "You don't need to go to that kind of place. Why don't you call your friends in Virginia and see what they can do?"

Francis agreed. He called the Hills, and they volunteered to go see the Speers and find out what could be done so that Toshimasa could leave for the United States.

A few days later he received a phone call. "Where have you been?" Captain Tagaki sounded very irritated and angry. "Don't you know you must report to me every morning?"

Toshimasa apologized, but then said, "I have decided to try to get a visa in another way. I'm not learning anything about the import-export business, and I don't see how all this will help me get to the United States."

The captain spoke, "But why didn't you come talk

to me if you didn't like your work? And you know, only I can give you a visa because you will be traveling as a businessman representing my company."

Toshimasa wanted to ask how he could play the role of a businessman when he didn't know much at all about the company, but he kept silent.

"I received a wire from the Speers," the captain continued. He said nothing for several seconds. Then, "I didn't mean for you to be unhappy. I did want you to be well prepared for the United States. Why don't you come see me, and we'll start working on your visa."

Toshimasa thanked him and hung up. Did the man really want to help him, or had the captain merely wanted a convenient personal servant for as long as he could manage to keep one? He didn't want to think about that.

The next day Captain Tagaki gave Toshimasa some papers and told him to go to the U.S. embassy. "Now put down on the paper that you are representing my company," the captain directed. "Say that you are taking newly developed navigation equipment to present to Captain Speer's company."

But that's a lie, Toshimasa wanted to say. I don't know anything about navigation systems, and you have taught me nothing about your business. But he dared not antagonize the captain. The captain continued, "Tell them you will be in the United States as a technical assistant for the next six months."

Toshimasa didn't like to, but did as he was instructed. The embassy granted him the visa, and he returned to the captain. "When can I leave?" he asked.

The captain studied some papers on his desk and mumbled, "Oh, next week."

Next week came, but when Toshimasa asked the

captain if he could arrange to leave, the captain got very angry and wouldn't discuss the matter with him. Toshimasa went home and got out the last letter from the Speers. That letter was dated a month before, and it contained the ticket Toshimasa needed. Now Toshimasa wondered whether he would ever get to use that ticket.

The next week Toshimasa again called the captain to ask him when he could leave for the United States. "He is on a business trip," the secretary informed him.

Hey! Toshimasa thought. Now is my chance! This is the perfect time to leave. He went to Tokyo and got an appointment with the vice-president, the captain's son. He didn't know how much the son knew about what had happened in the past several months, so he made a simple request. "Your father has granted me a visa so that I can serve as a company representative, and I would like to leave this evening."

The son answered, "Go ahead. I'll take care of it. My father won't be home until six o'clock this evening. I will tell him you decided to leave, and I'll check what he wants you to do."

"I really appreciate your help." Toshimasa shook the man's hand.

He raced home. Quickly he got out the tailor-made suits that hung in the closet, waiting for this moment. He looked at them as he packed—his grandmother had bought one of them for him, his parents another, and he had bought the other three himself. He would at least look the part of a businessman. His parents called together his friends, and they all headed for the Tokyo airport.

Just as they went through the door, the phone rang. The mayor of the town wanted to see Toshimasa for a few minutes. On the way to Tokyo, Toshimasa stopped at his office. "I wish you much success," the mayor said, shaking Toshimasa's hand and giving him something. Toshimasa was amazed to see $25. "Now let me make one final suggestion," the mayor said smiling. "Don't bring home a blue-eyed bride."

A large group gathered around Toshimasa as they waited in the airport. He looked at them. Each one meant much. Most of them represented his ties to his hometown. Father Joseph had been a trusted friend and counselor to him. His parents and his sisters stood there too. Other friends had also come for this special occasion. Toshimasa trembled with anticipation and the emotions that crowded in on him at this special moment. He wanted to leave, yet felt reluctant. He glanced at his watch. Only a half hour before his flight would leave.

Then he heard an angry shout. "Toshimasa!"

He turned. There came a furious Captain Tagaki striding down the hall. "You didn't get my permission to leave! Cancel your flight!"

Father Joseph stepped forward. "But, Captain, you know the Speers are anxious to have him there."

"It's none of your business!" Captain Tagaki shouted. "Just stay away from me. I will call Hawaii. I will tell them that you are not my agent."

Toshimasa wanted to shrink into nothingness. This had been his big moment, a time when all those people dear to him honored him by saying nice things, a time when his dream was coming true. What a humiliation! He glanced at his father and saw how much his father wanted to fight back. He held his breath. If his father quarreled with Captain Tagaki, all could be ruined. Then as he saw his father turn away he gave a sigh of relief and felt a surge of gratefulness for his father, whom he had feared and at times even hated.

Toshimasa heard the loudspeaker call his flight number. In desperation he turned to Captain Tagaki. He wanted to remind him that it was the Speer's money, not Captain Tagaki's, that had paid for the ticket. He wanted to ask him why he had been so seemingly unreasonable about letting him get a visa and leave. He wanted to know why he never got paid for those months of tedious work. But he asked none of those things. A tense minute passed. Finally the captain glared and, with an angry flick of his hand, disappeared.

Toshimasa let out a long breath. He had thought he would see a dream shattered right then and there. Then the tension broke. Laughter and tears surrounded him as they hurried him to the gate. An airline employee looked at his ticket and rushed him to the plane. "Hurry, they've been waiting for you."

He took a window seat, but could see little at that hour of the night. As the mist closed in he sat alone with his thoughts. I can't believe it, he kept saying to himself. Am I really going? Do I really want to go?

In the morning the plane touched down in Hawaii and then headed for the West Coast of the United States. Toshimasa studied his ticket. He had to get off in Seattle. Someone connected with Captain Tagaki's company would meet him.

The plane landed, and the stewardess spoke into the microphone. What did she say? Toshimasa wondered. Did she say Seattle? He tried to look out but couldn't see any signs. He got off and wandered around the airport. He decided to sit and wait. He sat, and waited, and waited some more. He couldn't believe that Captain Tagaki had finally gotten his revenge, but sure enough, nobody approached him. He heard the loudspeaker call his original flight number, so he decided to check at the desk once more.

"Can I help you?" the man at the counter spoke. Toshimasa stared. He had studied English, but not enough to be able to communicate here in the United States. Everyone seemed to have a different accent and spoke so fast. All he could think of saying was "Seattle." The man grabbed his ticket, gave it a quick glance, and then ran from behind the counter.

"Hurry! Your plane is leaving! This is Portland, not Seattle!" Toshimasa couldn't understand everything, but something certainly had gone wrong. The man shouted, "Wait, wait for this gentleman. He's supposed to be on the plane!"

Just as the attendant was closing the door he reached the plane and hurriedly boarded. What a close call! He could have been stranded in a strange city, with no one to call for help!

Before the next stop Toshimasa decided he would have to look carefully for the signs at the airports, because he couldn't understand announcements through the loudspeaker on the plane. They hurled the English language at him too fast and too noisily. When the plane landed he spotted the name of the city—Seattle—and to his relief, also Captain Tagaki's representative. After the visit he felt a little less nervous—one mission accomplished.

Back in the plane he felt himself tense up again. How many times would the plane land before he reached Washington, D.C.? Each time the plane taxied into an airport Toshimasa strained to read the signs. Five times he searched out the name of the airport and city. What a huge country! he thought. He toyed with his seatbelt and wiped his sweaty hands on his pants. He hoped he didn't look as nervous as he felt.

Finally he arrived in Virginia. This time he didn't have to check. There stood his friends, the Hills. What a great welcome! "Let's go get something to eat," Mrs. Hill urged. "You must be tired and hungry." They pulled into a McDonald's parking lot. Toshimasa had heard about American food and was anxious to try it. Later that night he wasn't so sure about it. He had eaten a hamburger, a milk shake, and french fries—a usual American meal, the Hills assured him. But as he sank into his bed he felt so sick. He couldn't tell for sure if the food had caused it or all the excitement or his weariness. But, it didn't matter, he decided. Tomorrow was his big day. Tomorrow he would see his new home. Tomorrow a new life would begin.

The next day the Hills drove him to Annapolis. Toshimasa marveled at the beautiful scenery, the naval academy, all the sights so strange to him. But he couldn't wait to see his new home. Finally the Hills pulled up to a huge gate. Inside the fenced-in area stood a mansion. "It looks like a castle," breathed Toshimasa.

They knocked on the door. Captain Speer met them and gave Toshimasa a hearty greeting. "You must be Francis," he said. That startled Toshimasa a little, but then he realized that because the Hills had made this contact for him, he would now be known as Francis because that's what they called him.

Captain Speer invited them into the grand house and showed them around. "Now, let me show you the grounds and other places," he said.

"Wait," the Hills told the captain. "Francis," Mrs. Hill said, "we have to leave." They hugged him and said, "We're sure you will be happy here."

Francis waved good-bye, then followed Captain Speer. He marveled at the beautiful grounds, the magnificient buildings in the neighborhood, the surrounding hills. "This is better than I expected," he thought.

Then he turned his attention to what the captain was saying. "Now this is the building where you will be staying." Toshimasa looked. There stood a gray, stark office building. The captain had gone through the door, and Toshimasa hurried after him. They rode the elevator silently to the top floor, and the captain got out. He gestured to a room on one side and said, "There's the school of music." He walked down the hall, opened the door, and walked in. Francis saw a storage room, with a tiny cubicle partitioned off that didn't reach the ceiling. The captain walked to it and motioned Francis inside. "Here," he said. "This is the room where you will be staying."

Francis saw an army cot in one corner, a tiny desk in another, and a chair in the middle. Only one dingy window let in feeble light.

The captain walked into the hall. He opened a door. "Here, you can use this bathroom. The employees use it during the day, and you can use it at night. Sorry, no hot water. But cold showers never hurt anyone." He patted Francis on the back, walked to the elevator, got in, and said over his shoulder, "Be sure you're at the house at 6:30 in the morning so you can get us breakfast."

Francis watched the elevator doors close. He stood, rooted to the spot. What had happened? After a minute he walked into the tiny cubicle, laid his luggage on the floor, and sat on the bed. This was his new home? Home! How strange! Surely there must be a mistake. Francis had a sinking feeling. He sank down on the cot and laid his head in his hands.

Chapter Six

The alarm rang. Francis reached to shut it off. He didn't really need the alarm, he realized now. He hadn't slept much. All night he brooded over what had happened the evening before. A foreboding filled him. He struggled out of the hard cot and headed for the bathroom across the hall. In the shower he shivered. He'd forgotten that Captain Speer had said, "No hot water—but cold showers never hurt anyone." It occurred to him that Captain Tagaki might approve of this austere life-style.

At 6:20 he studied himself in the old mirror in the bathroom. He tried to smile. Maybe if he really did his work well all would turn out for the best. After all, he had only been in America for about thirty hours.

He decided to walk down the stairs instead of taking the elevator. He didn't want to admit to himself that he felt reluctant about meeting the Speers this morning, but he didn't want to be late either. He crossed from the office building where he had spent the night and hurried to the mansion, about 200 feet away. Quietly he opened the back door and let himself in. He thought he remembered that Captain Speer had said something about "see you in the morning in the kitchen," but he wasn't sure.

A shrill voice interrupted his thoughts. "Ah, there you are. At last." Mrs. Speer, still dressed in a bathrobe, walked down the long hallway toward him. "You must always be on time," she said. "We will be taking our breakfast in our bedrooms. After I teach you, you will do this every morning."

Her stride echoed down the hall as she went toward the kitchen. Meekly, Francis followed her, a smile frozen on his face.

Mrs. Speer turned to face him. "Now, listen carefully. Nod if you understand what I am saying. The captain wants his egg boiled exactly three minutes." She paused. He nodded. She continued with instructions about preparing breakfast and then said, "Mrs. Nielsen comes in at 10:00 in the morning. She will prepare the other meals. You will be helping her serve them. She will feed you here in the kitchen." As she walked out of the door she said over her shoulder, "When you have finished serving our breakfast, I have other work for you to do."

Francis stood still for a moment in the large kitchen quiet and serene around him. The woman frightened him. Briefly, thoughts of his music education flitted through his head, but he shoved them aside as he began to prepare breakfast.

The first few days at the Speer mansion blended into one. Francis worked hard. Carefully he dusted the expensive and valuable antiques. He waxed the floor by hand and carefully shined the chandeliers. The brass and silver looked shiny, but Mrs. Speer demanded they be polished with unnecessary regularity. "They're going to wear out if I keep this up," Francis thought.

Then he had to care for the huge lawn. The captain instructed him on how to mow it and trim the edges.

"We must keep everything looking nice," he said. "After all, we are next to the governor's mansion." He pointed to a large white home some 400 feet away. For two days Francis pushed the mower around. He didn't mind keeping things looking nice. Only the pace bothered him, and he realized he would have to repeat the whole process next week.

When he rode the elevator to his stark cubicle for the night, he often wondered about his music. Finally he decided to ask Mrs. Speer about it. He would have preferred to talk to the captain, but Mrs. Speer seemed to be the one in charge. The captain only appeared at mealtimes and in the evening.

His chance came the next day. Mrs. Speer listed his day's work and said, "But first you will drive me downtown. I need to do some shopping."

Francis pulled the expensive English car into the driveway, and Mrs. Speer settled herself comfortably in the back seat. He wanted to talk to her, to practice his English, but fear always seemed to tangle his tongue. Finally he cleared his throat and glanced back at her. "Mrs. Speer," he began, and then hesitated.

"Yes, what is it?" she sounded annoyed.

Francis plunged in. "W-when can I begin studying music?" he stuttered, then felt angry with himself. He had little chance to practice English, and now the strain made him sound ignorant.

Mrs. Speer didn't say anything for long moments. Finally she said, "I have contacted the piano teacher. His office is on the same floor as your room. You can go see him about lessons."

Francis waited for more, but she sat back, silent once again. The Annapolis School of Music! he thought bitterly. He had seen the small area that contained only two studios. Captain Speer had assigned him the job of night watchman in return for his room and board, and Francis knew what type of business each floor of the office building contained. But, he said to himself, I'm not going to give up. I'll start with the lessons, and then maybe in a little while the Speers will see that I am serious and will send me to a real school. Deftly he pulled the elegant car into a parking space and assisted Mrs. Speer out.

After the first week Francis discovered that his job also included tending the garden. As he stooped to gather up the weeds he had just hoed, a shadow fell across the patch of cabbages. He looked up and saw a stooped, middle-aged man staring at him and thoughtfully smoking a pipe.

Francis grinned.

The man smiled back. "Hi!" he said. "You must be the new houseboy."

Francis grinned again and nodded.

"Well," the man went on, "so they got another one. Wonder how long you'll last! Are you Japanese?"

Francis nodded again, trying hard to understand and warming to the man's friendly tone.

"My name is Jim," the man informed him. He reached out a hand. Francis had been ready to bow, Japanese style, but he caught himself and grasped Jim's hand.

"What do you do here?" Francis wanted to know. He hoped Jim wouldn't laugh at his English. The only person he talked to much was Mrs. Nielsen, the Danish cook who fed him and sometimes corrected his English. Otherwise he just took orders and said little.

"I'm the live-in repairman." Jim tossed his head in the direction of the mansion. "You've seen their expensive junk; I keep it in shape. It's a museum in there!"

"I see," Francis ventured. He wanted to know more. It felt great to be talked to like a real person, not just a mute servant taking orders.

"How do you get along with Mrs. Speer?" Jim asked. Without waiting for an answer, he went on. "She's tough on help. Do you know that the record for any houseboy or household help staying is about half a year? We've had them from New York, from the Islands, another one from your own country. She doesn't give me a hard time because she respects what I do for her possessions, but otherwise, whew!" Jim rolled his eyes and shook his head.

"Why?" Francis wanted to know.

"Well, now, my friend, I don't really know. But I have an idea. Did you notice the pictures in the library? Two young men, a young woman, a young family? The two young men are sons. Both killed. Went to the naval academy, graduated top of their classes, and so on. They were to be great leaders of our country." Jim paused, reflecting. "The war took them. They have only their daughter and her family now, that's all."

Francis listened. He had wondered if the Speers had any children, because so far no one had visited that looked like children or grandchildren.

Jim continued his recital. "Maybe that made them bitter. Maybe that's why they're so hung up on all those antiques they own." He leaned toward Francis and said in a confidential tone. "Did you know they own most of the stores on main street—the souvenir shop, the laundromat, the antique store in that building, in fact that building itself." He pointed toward the place where Francis spent his nights. "Do you know how much rent they pick up—rent only?" He paused for effect. "Thousands and thousands of dollars each month. And what do they pay you?" he demanded.

"I don't know," Francis faltered. He had been afraid to ask, particularly since he thought the Speers would send him to school in return for the work he did.

"I can tell you." Jim looked important. "You'll get fifty bucks a month. You know that? Fifty bucks a month! Now try and do something with that!"

Francis looked startled, but Jim put a friendly arm around his shoulders and said, "Come on. You've worked long enough. Let's go take a break. If Mrs. Speer says anything, I'll handle it."

Jim was right. At the end of the month Francis held a check for fifty dollars in his hand. From this he had to pay for all his personal items such as deodorant, toothpaste, mouthwash. Then Francis discovered many costs he hadn't planned on. Even though the mansion had a huge, well-equipped laundry, Mrs. Speer refused him its use. He had to go to the laundromat and insert his own dimes and quarters. How would fifty dollars pay for all he needed?

He pocketed the check and decided to go talk to the piano teacher. "I would like to take lessons," he requested as they sat in the meagerly furnished studio.

"OK," the teacher answered. "I charge $5 a lesson. Can you pay that?"

Francis reacted in surprise. "I thought—" he didn't quite know how to phrase his reply. "I thought that Mrs. Speer would arrange to pay for my lessons." He tried to tell the teacher about the original agreement that brought him to the United States, but the man cut him off.

"No. No arrangement like that has been made with me."

Francis ponderd. "Five dollars a lesson?" he repeated incredulously.

"Yes."

The silence fell as the teacher fidgeted uneasily.

"I cannot pay," Francis said softly. "I only get fifty dollars a month. Your fee would amount to twenty or twenty-five dollars each month for lessons." He shook his head sadly. "How will I live?"

The teacher's face softened. "OK, let's make a deal. I'll give you lessons; in return you'll clean the studio—mop it, dust it, and put things in order. How does that suit you?"

Francis felt some relief. "Sure," he replied.

Well, at least he wouldn't be neglecting his study of music altogether. That night he sat down at the rickety table in his room and decided to answer the letters from home.

"Everything is fine," he wrote. "I'm studying music and the Speers are fine people, and—" His pen stopped, and he stared out into the dark night. How could he tell them what had really happened? He felt the pressure of having to live up to the expectations back home. After all, he had defied his parents. He had defied Captain Tagaki. He had a visa that entitled him to be in America under false circumstances. He rummaged through the papers in his battered briefcase and found the written agreement the Speers had sent him. Yes, he thought, they did promise to send me to school. Here it is. Now what can I do?

That night he couldn't sleep well. Usually he heard some noises during the night that he had to investigate as night watchman. But tonight, stifling the apprehensions he felt when he heard someone walking on the second floor, he remained silent on his cot. "What should I do about going to school?" he wondered. "What should I do?"

By morning his gloom still hadn't vanished. During the noon meal he sat silent in the kitchen while Mrs.

Nielsen heaped his plate with food, barely managing to smile at the kindly woman. If it weren't for her and Jim, he thought, life would surely be lonely. Mrs. Nielsen bustled about the kitchen, a tiny form about seventy years old, her sweet round face framed by white hair. When she sat down with her own plate he decided he'd try to forget his miserable feelings and chat with her as was their custom. Just then the door opened. Mrs. Speer stared at his dinner plate, frowned, and said, "That's too much food!" Then she left the kitchen.

Francis later noticed that his plate held smaller servings and that the good rapport he had with Mrs. Nielsen had been chilled a little. The poor woman was under orders to limit his food! From then on, each day after working hard in the house and yard and running errands he went to bed at night with a gnawing feeling in his stomach.

Often as he chauffered the Speers around he wanted to turn and scream at them, "Why are you doing this?" But realizing he couldn't do such a shocking thing, he simply stared ahead and drove in silence.

Jim's friendship kept him going. Each day the older man looked for Francis and chatted with him. Often he took Francis to the park, shopping, or to his daughter's home. Through him, Francis learned much about American life-style. Francis thought that perhaps Jim felt loneliness too. Whatever the case, he appreciated Jim's warm, outgoing style and the time Jim took to show him around. That made it possible for him to face the long list of duties each day. No letup in that, he realized.

One day as Francis passed through the first floor of the building where he slept, the manager of Captain Speer's navigation systems business met him. "Say, I understand you're a Catholic too," he said.

Francis replied. "Yes, but I haven't been to church lately, not since I got here."

The man nodded understandingly. "Why don't you come to church with us?"

"Sure!" Francis grasped the man's hand eagerly. Then his face sobered. "Do you think the Speers will let me?"

"We'll work that out."

On succeeding Sundays the manager and his family picked up Francis and took him to church and after the services brought him back to the mansion to work. The Sunday-morning worship provided a relief for Francis from the drudgery of the week's work—along with the orchestra rehearsals he attended every Thursday night. His piano teacher had told him that the Annapolis symphony orchestra was holding auditions. Francis tried out for the trumpet section and placed third chair. So each week Francis had an additional three-hour break. After the rehearsals some of the other musicians often invited him to go for a drink with them. Francis liked these times. He never drank much, but he enjoyed sitting around the table with the other men and listening while they talked about music, politics, and life in general.

Among his new acquaintances was Mrs. Price, who owned the antique shop on the first floor of the business building. Each day she greeted Francis, and soon she invited him into the shop for a chat. Francis began to help her some in the shop, particularly with the oriental antiques. One day she said to him, "You must meet the Leonards. They collect Japanese antiques."

"Who are they?"

"He's vice-president of International Bank, the largest national bank in Maryland."

Soon after they met Francis, the Leonards invited him to their home for dinner. When Francis asked Mrs. Speer's permission to be absent for an evening, she looked surprised. "Where are you going?" she demanded.

"The Leonards have invited me to dinner this evening," Francis answered.

Mrs. Speer's face hardened. "Oh," was all she said in reply.

The Leonards were gracious and before long became his close friends. A few meetings later they asked "What are you doing at the Speers?"

"I came to the United States to study music," Francis explained, "but I'm working long hours as a house and yardboy. I only get a small allowance, and I can't go to school. It costs several thousand dollars to go to music school."

The Leonards looked at each other then back at Francis. "Why, if you came to study, you must study! What can we do to help you?"

Eventually they decided to talk to the Speers. "I'm sorry," Mrs. Leonard said to Francis after the meeting, "but it wasn't a pleasant talk. Mrs. Speer is quite adamant that you are obligated to work for them." She took on a thoughtful look, "Do you have any ideas on what we can do before we try anything really drastic?"

Francis thought. Could the Hills help? He hadn't told them about his predicament. They probably thought he had a nice room in the mansion and would probably begin music study soon. Whenever he wrote them he said the same things as he did to his family and friends at home: "All's fine!" He didn't want to complain, and of course there was the matter of the visa. Also, he didn't have much money. "I don't know," he finally answered.

In the meantime other people took an interest in Francis. One day as he left the laundromat he bumped into a woman coming down the street. "Oh, excuse me," he apologized.

"No problem," the woman said with a laugh. She stopped and looked him over. "Say! you're the Speer's houseboy, aren't you?"

Francis nodded. They began to talk. Francis discovered that her husband taught at the naval academy and that she also liked music, especially dance and ballet. She promised to invite him to her home.

Again Francis had to ask Mrs. Speer's permission to leave for an evening. She frowned. "How did you make a connection like that?"

Francis tried to explain, but the whole affair annoyed Mrs. Speer. "People should ask my permission before they invite you anywhere," she fumed.

Francis's circle of friends grew—a banker and his family, a lawyer, a professor and his wife, even a general of the United States army. Besides them, he had friends at the local Red Cross office. To try to supplement his meager monthly allowance, Francis had taken a janitorial job at that office. The secetaries treated him kindly, and one of them took a special interest in him. "Oh," she said at their first meeting, "so you're the Speer's current prisoner!"

Francis first felt sheepish, but then saw that she meant the remark as a joke. Maybe she realizes what it's like, he thought. Many people had expressed either curiosity or sympathy when they discovered he worked for the Speers. That offered some comfort, but did little to ease his daily chores.

Jane, the secretary at the Red Cross office, would often call him into her office and say, "Now, it's time for a break. You sit down here. Talk to me."

She began asking him all kinds of questions, especially about Japan. Frequently she interrupted him by saying, "No, that's not the right way to say it," and she corrected his English.

After some weeks went by she said, "Say, there's a shower with hot water upstairs. Feel free to use it. There's a bed there, too, if you want to use it sometimes."

In December Francis decided to visit the Hills. It had been about half a year since he had seen them. When he arrived at their home, Mrs. Hill took one look at him and exclaimed, "What's happened to you?"

Francis wasn't sure what she meant.

"You're so skinny! How much weight have you lost?" She got out the bathroom scales, and he weighed himself. Only 132 pounds! That surprised them both. He had lost over 40 pounds.

"You must eat," Mrs. Hill exclaimed. As she fed him a huge meal in the kitchen, she plied him with questions. Gradually Francis spilled out the whole story.

"We must do something. You've got to leave there." Mrs. Hill got very perturbed. "They're violating the agreement on which the visa was granted!"

"No! No!" Francis hurriedly answered. "I don't want to cause any problem. And I'm still afraid of what Captain Tagaki might do. Besides, if I get into trouble, I'll be sent back to Japan, and I don't have any money. I couldn't come back again. Don't say anything," he pleaded.

Mrs. Hill looked doubtful. "All right," she agreed. "But can't you think of something we can do?"

That question reminded Francis of what Mrs. Leonard had asked—almost in the same words.

"Maybe," he said, "Maybe you could talk to my

friends the Leonards. They might have thought of a solution."

The visit with his American family had boosted Francis's spirits, but when he returned to the mansion, depression hit him once again. Mrs. Speer increased his work but not his allowance.

A few evenings later he sat down wearily on his hard cot and put his head in his hands. The problems of the last six months overwhelmed him. Was life worth living? he wondered. Maybe dying would be better. All kinds of thoughts and memories rushed through his head, and he couldn't hold it back any longer. He burst into tears.

After some time his sobs subsided. He didn't know how long he had cried, but he didn't feel much better. He spotted his trumpet. He grabbed it and blasted out sounds as long as his lips could stand it. Then he rushed to the studio and banged on the piano until his arms and fingers ached. Slowly he returned to his cot. Totally exhausted, he knelt by the bed and prayed, "God if there's any way out of all these troubles, please help me!" Finally he fell into a restless sleep.

The next morning the depression hadn't lifted, but he felt somewhat better when he chatted with Jim and when Mrs. Nielsen slipped him two extra slices of bread. They reminded him of all the people who had been kind to him during the past six months. Maybe they could think of something, even though he didn't see any way out of his predicament.

Mrs. Leonard did have an idea. "Your friends the Hills and I have talked. We're working on a plan."

Francis's spirit lifted. Why should he be depressed when so many fine people cared about his future?

Mrs. Leonard continued. "We have an application for you at the music school of The Catholic University of America in Washington, D.C. And you must go and audition."

Francis thanked her, filled out the application, and made an appointment for an audition. When he told Mrs. Speer that he would take a day off and go to Washington to audition at a university, she looked shocked. Her tense look haunted Francis as he left for the audition, but he soon forgot everything when he arrived at the university.

But Francis failed the audition. He tried to explain to the dean of the school of music, "I've had a very bad cold for the past week and haven't touched the instrument. Can I have a second chance?"

The dean considered his request and then said, "Why don't you come back in a month?"

Francis agreed eagerly. On the bus back to Annapolis he slid down on the seat in misery. Suddenly he sat up straight. Was it possible that Mrs. Speer had something to do with his failure? He couldn't be certain, of course, but with her influence and money—. He would probably never know, but he vowed to practice very hard and pass the audition the next time.

After the second audition, Francis was summoned to the assistant dean's office. There sat Mrs. Hill and Mrs. Leonard. The dean spoke, "You've passed the audition. How much can you pay for your schooling?"

Francis felt relief and despair at the same time. He glanced at the smiling Mrs. Hill.

The dean went on. "Can you pay $75 at first?"

"Yes," Francis quickly replied. "I've saved that much."

"Fine," the dean said. "We will be able to offer you a scholarship, and you can work as my assistant. Because of your lack of language skills, you should take only eight credit hours."

"We'll pay for your books and music," Mrs. Hill added.

Francis sat still, overwhelmed. Then a horrible thought hit him. "What about my visa?" he inquired.

"Oh, yes," the dean replied. "You must have the proper permission to stay in this country."

Some tense days passed while Mrs. Leonard and Mrs. Hill made many phone calls. Finally they discovered that Francis could keep the business visa he had renewed a few months before and be a part-time student. Later he could change his status to full-time student.

"Phew! What a scary time!" Francis said when Mrs. Hill told him the news. He scarcely knew how to thank these wonderful people. What miracles they had done for him. Then he wondered—had God heard his desperate prayer?

When Francis received his acceptance letter from the Catholic University along with the notification about the scholarship, he showed them to Mrs. Speer.

Mrs. Speer scowled. "You can't do this! We paid the air fare to bring you here. You owe us that!"

But Francis realized that, considering the long hours he had worked and the meager allowance he had received, he had more than paid for his air fare.

Mrs. Speer remained adamant, so Francis began to plan. A few nights later he packed. The next day he would take the captain to the airport in Washington, D.C. Somehow he would make his getaway. Quietly he stole out of the building and made his way to the mansion's garage. He pulled the car keys from his pocket. How fortunate that the captain provided him with a chauffeur's set of keys. He unlocked the trunk, put in his belongings, closed the lid as softly as he could, and crept back to his room.

Chapter Seven

On the way to the airport, Francis chose his words carefully. He liked the captain, but now he well realized that Mrs. Speer controlled the household and the money while the captain pursued his own interests—thinking and studying and coming up with new ideas and inventions.

"Captain," Francis began.

Captain Speer looked up from the papers he was working on.

"Sir, when you return from your trip, you will have to drive home yourself," Francis continued.

Now he had the captain's full attention. "What do you mean?" Captain Speer asked.

"I am leaving your employ," Francis explained. "I came to the United States to study. Your wife will not agree to my going to school. But that's what I really came to do. By the way, all my belongings are in the trunk. My friends the Hills will be picking me up at the airport."

"I'm very surprised," the captain said. "I didn't know about your plans. I thought you had come to work. You see," he tried to clarify his statements, "my wife handles all the domestic staff. I wasn't aware. Can I help in any way?"

Francis shook his head. He realized that the captain's intentions might be good, but in the long run the man would probably forget about him, or his wife would not allow money to be spent for Francis's education.

"I'm really sorry about what has happened," the captain apologized. "If I had known, I might have prevented it."

Francis drove on in silence. The tension slowly left him. The captain hadn't given him a hard time, and he appreciated that. At the same time, he felt bad because of the friends he left behind. He hadn't even been able to say good-bye to them. He thought of Jim, whose warm friendship he would miss. He hoped Jim would understand why he had to leave with no farewell. Now that the nightmare of the past seven months had ended, he remembered especially the friends who had done so much for him—the Leonards, the antique shop owner, Jane from the Red Cross, the professor's wife. He hoped someday he could come back and visit them.

At the airport Francis parked the car and helped the captain with his luggage. The captain shook Francis's hand. "Good luck," he said.

Then Francis spotted the Hills driving through the parking lot. The emotions he had felt over the past seven months washed over him. He felt such a tremendous relief, that when they greeted each other he could hardly say anything. He just grinned.

Francis appreciated his American family. He realized they lived under some tension, because Captain Hill flew in and out of Vietnam, fighting in the war there. And he also knew they didn't have much extra money, especially now with two daughters in college.

Each morning Francis took a bus and rode for an hour and a half to get to Catholic University in Washington, D.C. He liked the performance groups and lessons, but theory class gave him problems. He had learned the German and Italian terms, but now the English vocabulary puzzled him. Besides, his teacher, a Frenchman, spoke with a heavy accent and usually chewed on a cigar. Francis could hardly understand him, and he failed to appreciate the extra attention the teacher paid to him. The teacher would throw the first question of every new chapter at Francis, and then he'd say, "Come on, Frank. Take your time but hurry up." Francis got more nervous with each class period.

For several hours each day he worked for the assistant dean, running his errands, getting the coffee, photocopying. But he liked this work, not only because the dean treated him well, but also because he got quickly acquainted with the other professors. Their friendliness impressed him.

But the long trip to and from the university wore him out. He wished he could work out some way to live near the school, but came up with no solution.

A few weeks later he met a seminary student from Japan, Brother Naoki, studying to be a priest at Catholic University. During their conversation Brother Naoki said, "There's a Japanese students' meeting coming up at the seminary just a few blocks away. We get together once in a while and socialize. Would you like to come and meet with us?"

Francis agreed quickly. He always liked meeting new people, particularly from his own country and of his own faith. A few evenings later he walked to the seminary. When he got there he stood in awe, studying the beautiful modern building with stained-glass windows. Inside, he admired the paintings and works of art from many different countries.

After the meeting, the director of the seminary met Francis and began to ask some questions. "Where do you live, and what are you doing now?" he asked.

Francis explained, "I live with an American family in Virginia, and every day I commute to Catholic University. I'm a student there."

"What a long way to travel!" the priest exclaimed. "Why don't you come live with us? We've got a room available."

Francis only smiled politely, not sure he understood everything, then said good-night and left.

When he arrived home that night he told Mrs. Hill about his visit with the Japanese students at the seminary. Then he added, "I think the superior offered me a room. But I couldn't understand him very well."

Mrs. Hill looked surprised. "How much did he say it would cost you?"

Francis didn't know.

"I'll call tomorrow and find out what he really meant," Mrs. Hill offered.

The next day she phoned the director of the seminary and asked, "Francis says you offered him a room. How much will it cost?"

"Nothing," the priest answered. "It's free."

"Why would you do that?" Mrs. Hill asked, astonished. "We would be willing to pay some. We can't come up with too much money, but we are willing to pay room and board."

"No," the priest replied. "That's not necessary. We have a room available anyway and many hungry young people to feed. It doesn't make any difference if Francis joins us. Besides," he added, "it would be good to have him here as a lay brother among all these young candidates for priesthood."

"That's wonderful!"

"We have missions in Japan, you know," the priest continued. "He can teach us about that country and its language. And he can help around the place just like the other brothers—cleaning up and washing dishes."

"This is good news!" Mrs. Hill could hardly contain her enthusiasm.

When the weekend came, Francis packed his belongings once again, and the Hills drove him to Washington, D.C. They attended the Sunday-morning mass at the seminary, and then the director showed them around. They toured the Japanese garden, then went to the recreation room downstairs. Immediately Francis spotted the ping-pong table and noticed the adjoining stereo room. They looked at the music room, where Francis could practice. The director also showed them the laundry room and the barbershop.

Finally the director took them to Francis's room. Francis couldn't help exclaiming, "What a nice place!" After his seven months in the stark cubicle at Speer's office building, this seemed like heaven. He'd be comfortable in this nicely furnished room, with heat and air conditioning.

"We're just like brothers here," the director said. "We do have a strict schedule, and no one is allowed in anyone else's room. But," he said as he turned to Francis and smiled, "there's no rule that brothers can't visit a lay person. You will no doubt have many visitors."

Francis quickly adjusted to the seminary schedule. The time he saved by not commuting he used in studying and taking extra jobs. At six o'clock in the evening he met with the brothers for supper. He shared their recreation time until seven-thirty when the others went to their rooms to study and pray. Since Francis could have visitors, brothers soon began to find his room a nice place to congregate, sometimes staying until three or four in the morning.

During the social times the brothers often drank and

urged Francis to join them. He hesitated, remembering his father's drinking bouts. But when they teased him, he drank a small glass of wine with them, declining to go beyond that. He did like his pipe, though. A friend bought Francis his first one and urged him to try many different tobacco brands. "Hey, I want you to start pipe smoking, because it's really good for you," he said. Francis got nauseated, but eventually he began to like the smell and especially the feel of a pipe in his hand and mouth. From then on, when studying, reading, or just relaxing, he kept the pipe in his hand and found himself smoking it more and more.

The brothers invited Francis to participate in everything they did—sports, picnics, visiting the sick or poor. People in the neighborhood began to call him Brother Francis. He felt like a seminarian and sometimes had to remind himself that he was not Brother Francis. He enjoyed the 5:00 a.m. daily worships, the lunchtime mass, and the evening vespers. These times of meditation brought back memories of Buddhist temples back in Japan.

Francis also participated in the musical activities of the church. Often the priest asked him to compose music to fit the English text, now that a decree had been passed eliminating the Latin-only mass. As part of the service, the priest had to sing the chant. When a new father came, he had a difficult time singing in tune, so he told Francis, "I can't sing. Why don't you do the part?"

Francis rather liked the idea. It gave him a more active part in the service, and he knew he could chant better than the priest. He dressed in the priest's robes and learned how to bless the congregation. After the services, many members came up to Francis and said, "Thank you, Father. That was beautiful."

The director overheard these compliments and said to Francis, "Yes, you'd make a great priest! Think about it."

Francis finished the semester with good grades and received another scholarship. Because students could take a free class if they could maintain a 3.0 grade average, Francis determined to keep up his grades. Taking a free class would ease the financial pressure somewhat.

When summer came Francis found a job at the National Press Club in downtown Washington. On his first day at the job as a busboy he wrestled a cart loaded with cases of alcoholic beverage. He struggled to get it over a hump, pushing and pulling. All of a sudden a whole case of beer fell off and smashed to the floor.

"Oh, no!" Francis breathed. "And the most expensive German beer besides!"

He held his breath when he saw the boss approaching. He knew he'd probably get a scolding, but hoped he wouldn't be fired. But the boss looked at the mess and said, "Hey, when you get all this picked up and cleaned, then I'll show you how to go over the humps." Francis sighed in relief.

Each day he had to make sure the bar had a sufficient supply of drinks and ice. When it closed at 2:00 a.m., he had to scrub the floor, clean up the bar and tables, and set out clean glasses for the next day.

While working at the National Press Club he watched the reporters. Their ability to gulp down glass after glass of alcohol amazed him, but their talk interested him even more. So this was where many reporters met their news sources—news happened here! He listened carefully, fascinated by being so close to reporters whose stories appeared in the papers the next day.

At the end of the summer Francis realized he couldn't keep up with the hectic pace of his job and be a student too, so he quit his job. On his last day at work, the president of International Telephone and Telegraph, also a member of the club, called for attention and began a speech.

"This young man," he said to the group, "has been working very hard here. We've been watching him, and he's a good fellow. We don't have lots of money, but if each of us gives just a little bit, we can give him some money." He passed around the hat, and the money poured in. Then he handed it to Francis and said, "If there's anything we can do to help you, just give us a call." Francis was at a loss for words. He tried to thank the group, but they nonchalantly brushed off his thanks. At home that evening he counted over $200.

After school resumed, a classmate who directed a church choir in a Catholic church invited him to come as a guest conductor. That pleased Francis; he hadn't done that type of thing since he left Japan.

His conducting didn't go unnoticed. When the priest of that church transferred to another, he called Francis. "I liked the way you directed and handled the kids at my former church. Will you come and be music director at my new church, the Church of the Little Flower, in Bethesda? It's the biggest church in the area, and the wealthiest. All the important people come here."

Francis didn't need much of a sales pitch. He liked to conduct, and the possibility of a job pleased him. But he asked, "Don't you already have a music director?"

"Well, yes," the priest answered. "But we like the way you direct and handle the choir, and we'd like to have you. Let's meet for lunch and talk about it."

The next day the monsignor took Francis to the Mayflower dining room and ordered a fancy meal. Then he began to describe the job. "You will have an excellent budget—$12,000 with which to hire musicians and buy music. I want you to conduct the adult choir, of course, and to develop two new choirs, a boys' choir and one for teenagers. Our music director will stay as organist. He won't give you any trouble."

Francis didn't take long to think about it. How could he refuse such an offer? "Fine," he said.

"You won't regret it," the priest sounded pleased. "The salary is good, the church is famous, and you will have everything you want."

At the first rehearsal for the adult choir Francis began to realize it wouldn't be as simple as the priest had described. The choir dearly loved the former music director, now relegated to the organ, and resented this strange foreigner who tried to make them learn music they didn't like and found too hard.

Francis sensed their resentment and rebellion. One soprano who stood in the front and sang louder than the rest also complained louder than anyone else. No matter what music Francis handed out, Mrs. Ambrose would say, "We can't do this kind of music!" After the rehearsal she came to Francis and said, "You are really mean!" Francis wanted to tell her the same, but decided otherwise.

Then Francis began to hold auditions for the new choirs the priest wanted him to organize. He listened to what seemed like over a hundred wiggly, lively, mischievous fourth, fifth, and sixth grade boys. One little boy, Ned, had a good voice and Francis let him join. Before long, however, he regretted it. After a particularly trying session, Francis said to Ned, "Sorry, but I can't have you in the choir."

The next day Francis received a note. It read simply, "If there is any way you can allow Ned back in the choir, I would appreciate it. Mrs. Muskie."

Francis had many little boys to choose from and didn't have to put up with disruptors, he decided. But the monsignor didn't take this event as calmly. "Francis," he said, "you can't do this! Don't you realize who these people are?"

Francis shrugged. He hadn't heard the name.

"Ned is the son of U.S. Senator Muskie."

Now that meant something! Francis hadn't gotten involved in politics at all, but even he realized *senator* indicated a high post in the government.

"Francis, you've got to let him back in," the priest ordered.

Francis shook his head. "No, I've got to stick with what I said. Next year he can audition again."

The monsignor flung out his arms helplessly, looked heavenward, and left.

The naughty choirboy situation didn't disturb Francis, but the attitude of his adult choir did. Especially Mrs. Ambrose. She acted like his worst enemy, always critical and outspoken. Finally he decided to do something. Maybe his choir members didn't like him, but he could like them. He would pay each one a visit. First on his list was Mrs. Ambrose. The chilly atmosphere in her home didn't help any, but when he showed her daughter how to play a certain passage on the piano, Mrs. Ambrose warmed up a bit. And when he offered to coach her son on the trumpet, she thawed even more. Eventually Mrs. Ambrose became his strongest supporter, and Francis had won a victory.

That fall auditions took place once again for the boys' choir. This time Mrs. Muskie accompanied Ned. This made Francis uneasy until she said, "That was a great lesson for my son. My husband is always on the road, and Ned has a tendency to be spoiled. You did the right thing. If you can consider him for this year, we would appreciate it."

So Ned returned to the choir, and Francis discovered what truly nice people the Muskies were. Once after mass, when the boys' choir had sung, they sat down with him and told him how much they appreciated the good music. Then Senator Muskie said, "If I go to the White House—if I win the presidency—would you consider becoming the family music teacher?"

Francis's mouth dropped open. He vaguely remembered the group of men that accompanied the Muskies to church, but hadn't attached much significance to it. Of course secret-service men were hard to miss as they stood stiffly at the church entrances, but Francis hadn't realized that this ordinary church member was campaigning to be President of the United States.

After that, Francis became more conscious of the "big names" who attended the Church of the Little Flower. He watched as Mr. Colby helped older people or members in wheelchairs, and then learned this man worked as CIA director.

The dedication of many of these church members impressed Francis, and he did think about becoming a priest. "It's a good life," he said to himself. But other things began to bother him. At the seminary, brothers often confided in him during their late-night talks, and Francis began to notice the high dropout rate. Some of the materialism and favoritism he noticed at his own church puzzled him, but then he rationalized that maybe this wasn't true in all churches. Even so, he couldn't come to a firm decision about entering the priesthood. Something kept him from it.

In the middle of his third year at the university Francis left the seminary. For two and a half years the brothers had shared their material goods and friendship with Francis, and now someone else needed his room. Francis didn't mind, although he would miss the fellowship. He soon found a comfortable apartment and helped pay for his rent by acting as caretaker.

While in his senior year, Francis took a woodwind methods course. At the beginning of every new class, Francis observed the others in the class, since people interested him.

He noticed a girl across the room. Instead of being dressed in jeans and a T-shirt, like most of the other students, she wore a simple but attractive dress. Hmmm, Francis thought, a nun taking advantage of the new rules in dress. He turned back to his music.

Chapter Eight

Francis enjoyed woodwind class because these instruments were among his favorites. He remembered his childhood, when he started to play the flute, when his parents refused him an instrument of his own, even when his teacher offered to pay. Since then he had also learned to play the clarinet. The teacher noticed that fact and said, "Why don't you help some of the students who can't play?" So Francis would meet with the others and teach them the fingerings and how to play the instruments. At times the girl he thought must be a nun joined these special-help groups.

Francis next spotted Nancy in a philosophy of education course. A priest taught that class, and often Nancy would engage him in spirited discussions about Christian education. Francis had never heard the term "Christian education," and he marveled at Nancy's knowledge and courage to defend her views in front of a large class. But when she said, "I'm a Seventh-day Adventist," Francis wondered, "What's a Seventh-day Adventist?"

Then the teacher assigned a project. "You will have to go visit a board of education meeting and write a report."

John, a friend of Francis and a trumpet player in the

Air Force Band, suggested, "Let's go together and take Nancy and my wife. Maybe Lori might want to come too—that includes all of the music majors in this class."

The group sat at the board meeting for several hours, until finally John whispered, "This is too boring! Let's go to my house and get something to eat!"

After that Francis and the others often got together to study for tests in the education class, but the study sessions frequently ended up as parties. John's wife usually prepared fantastic food, John and Francis got out their pipes, and the conversation turned to more exciting things than test preparation. During one of these sessions, after the group had discussed religion for a while, Nancy turned to Francis and said, "Why don't you come to my church with me?"

Francis replied, "Well, I'm curious enough! I would probably not mind going."

"Good!" Nancy answered. "I'll meet you on Saturday morning."

"Sunday morning," Francis corrected.

"No," Nancy said, "Saturday is when Seventh-day Adventists go to church."

Francis smiled, amused. "OK!" He never minded a new adventure.

On Saturday morning Nancy led Francis into the large Sligo Church in Takoma Park, Maryland, a suburb of Washington, D.C. Francis looked around in surprise. So many well-dressed people, most of them holding Bibles in their hands! He knew, of course, about the Bible. On Sundays and devotion times short passages from the Epistles or Gospels were read in his church, but he had never read the Bible much for himself. And the noise bothered him. He noticed all the church members greeting each other, shaking hands, even hugging. Sometimes children screamed. This lack of reverence appalled Francis. In his own church the people who did attend walked in quietly and never said a word during the service. Then the singing began. He looked around in amazement. At his church, when he tried to get the congregation to sing, he told them that hymn singing was praise to God and therefore needed a joyful, loud expression, but all he heard in response was a small sound. He had never heard singing like he heard it now—full, loud, in harmony, and with a lot of spirit. By the time the sermon began, Francis thought, "This isn't bad!" But now another surprise—the man who got up to speak looked just like everyone else. He didn't wear any robes like a priest. He just stood up and spoke to the people. Francis started glancing at his watch. He liked the man's style, but how long would he preach? In his church sermons lasted only ten or fifteen minutes. Thirty minutes passed. The preacher still talked on, so Francis settled back and continued to listen.

"Well, what did you think?" Nancy asked after church.

"Lots of surprises," Francis answered.

"Will you come again?" Nancy wanted to know.

"Um, maybe." Francis had to get used to this new experience. He didn't want to make any rash promises.

A few weeks later Francis received an invitation to dinner by Nancy's landlord. He accepted; he seldom refused a chance to meet interesting people and eat good food too.

Before the meal, the landlord opened the Bible, read a passage, and then prayed. This ceremony astonished Francis. At the seminary that type of ritual often took place before a meal, but he had never seen it done in a private home. He listened to the prayer: "And we are grateful for friends, Lord, and that Francis can be here with us. Bless him, and now we pray for a blessing on this meal. Amen."

Francis didn't quite know how to act. Seldom had he heard his name mentioned in prayer. When he turned his attention to the food on the table, he noticed some of it looked strange. "What is this?" he whispered to Nancy while talk swirled around them.

"Vegetarian meat," she whispered back.

Vegetarian meat! What a contradiction in terms! In Japan he ate mostly pickled vegetables, fish, and rice, and at the seminary the menu ordinarily contained beef, and fish on Fridays. But vegetarian meat!

One day when Francis called Nancy, he could tell she had been crying, "What's the matter?" he asked, concerned.

"My dog!" she sobbed. "My dog got killed!"

Francis hurried over to the apartment, tried to comfort her, and together they went to a kennel to pick out a new dog. After that they frequently got together to walk the new dog in the park. These times were good for lots of conversation, and often the talk turned to religion and Seventh-day Adventist beliefs.

Francis had never met anyone so straightforward and honest as Nancy. These character traits attracted him to her more and more. He didn't believe in her church, but he had to admire anyone who was so committed to a set of beliefs. She refused, for example, to play in concerts on her Sabbath. Though the director of her orchestra understood, Francis didn't. "I don't know what I'd do with you if you were in my orchestra!" he fumed. "I'd probably kick you out!"

Nancy hid none of what she believed and freely expressed her reasons for believing. Her faithfulness to the church impressed him.

During the next several months the friendship continued to grow. Then came the day when Francis said, "Let's get married."

"Do you think we can work out our differences in religion?" Nancy wanted to know. "I do appreciate your obvious concern for spiritual matters—something which means a great deal to me, by the way—but you know we can't agree on which day to worship."

"Oh, I think so," Francis sounded optimistic. "We can usually discuss things without too much conflict."

Nancy didn't say anything for a few minutes, and Francis studied her. His eyes narrowed as he pondered whether she thought about the eventual disapproval of this marriage by her church and Seventh-day Adventist friends. He vaguely remembered hearing something about "being unequally yoked together," but that didn't seem to apply to them. After all, as Nancy had pointed out, they were both Christians. Wasn't that the only thing that mattered?

The next time they met, Nancy told Francis what happened when she broke the news concerning their engagement to her parents. "My father clapped his hand to his forehead," she related, "and moaned, 'This is my second Pearl Harbor!' I don't know if you realize it, but he fought during the second world war—and fought the Japanese."

Francis chuckled. "Has anyone else said anything about our getting married?"

Nancy's face grew serious. "When I casually mentioned it to my pastor, he counseled me to be sure that we worked out our religious differences before we actually got married." She paused. "You know, in general my church disapproves of this kind of thing. And if you aren't an Adventist, we can't get married in the Adventist church," she informed Francis.

"Does it matter to you where we get married?" Francis inquired.

"I just don't want to go to a justice of the peace or something so unimaginative," Nancy answered. "I do want a church wedding, don't you?"

"Hmm," Francis nodded, not willing to commit himself. "I told Dr. Frederickson we were getting married. You know what worried him most?"

"No, what?"

"Our cultural differences. He said he hopes we realize what problems we might have because I'm Japanese and you're American."

Nancy looked away. "That's something else to consider, I guess, besides our different viewpoints on which day to worship!"

Francis sat silently for a minute, then asked, "Do you still want to get married?" Again he wondered what she really thought about whenever they talked of marriage. He knew by now that most of her church members had some strong convictions against marrying a non-Adventist, as they put it.

Nancy turned to face him. "Yes," she answered. "Yes, I do. We'll work it out when you come to meet my family in Pennsylvania next week."

Francis grinned. Apparently those strong convictions didn't bother her that much. He felt relieved. Now they could go ahead with their plans.

In Pennsylvania, Nancy and Francis discussed their situation with other members of Nancy's family. Her sister frowned. "Since you can't get married in the Adventist church," she said, "what will you do?"

Before Nancy could answer, her Catholic brother-in-law broke in, "We'll help you. I'll talk to my priest, and he can counsel you. You can probably get married in the Catholic church."

The next day Francis and Nancy faced the priest in his study. "Are you a member of the Catholic Church?" he asked Francis.

"Yes." Francis told him details of his conversion in Japan.

"We will need your baptismal certificate," the priest said.

"But I don't have one. We'll have to write to Japan, and that will take a long time." Francis sounded worried.

The priest shrugged. "Ordinarily we wouldn't be able to marry you in our church, but I can get special permission from the bishop—if you have your baptismal certificate."

Francis glanced at Nancy. He guessed she didn't want to wait any more than he did.

After they left the office Francis turned to Nancy. "Do you want to wait for the certificate to come from Japan?"

"Yes," she responded. "I do want to get married in a church."

Francis wondered whether she felt bad about not getting married in her own church, or at least some Adventist church, but decided against asking. She had already told him that she couldn't get married in her church unless he became a member. That was something he certainly didn't want to consider.

Time lagged while they waited for the needed baptismal certificate, but about three months later it finally came. Late one Friday evening in a candlelight service in the Catholic church in Nancy's hometown they said their vows.

After the marriage they moved to Francis's apartment in Washington, D.C., where Francis finished his senior year, then began his master's program in conducting. Although counseled against it, he determined to finish that degree in just one year. He had no money to spend beyond a year.

A year later Francis graduated with the coveted degree and began the job-hunting chores. Francis decided to talk to Nancy once more about an idea he had. "Shall we go back to Japan? You know it's been my dream to become a high school teacher and band director. I'd like to go to my hometown."

"No." Nancy kept her attention focused on the dishes she was washing. "I don't want to go there for good."

"But you could teach there too."

"No," Nancy murmured. "I'm afraid I wouldn't fit into the traditional social structure. I'm afraid of doing something that would offend or hurt your parents. Besides, I don't think I could manage to live with your parents as the customary 'first son's wife.' "

Francis sighed. He knew that the oldest son and his wife were expected to return home and live in the same house as the parents. The wife had to act almost as a servant to her parents-in-law and her husband. Every paycheck would be turned over to the parents, and he and Nancy would receive an allowance from that check. After ten years, the restrictions would loosen somewhat, but they would still be expected to live in the same house until the parents died. Francis realized he probably wouldn't change Nancy's mind. The cultural differences in relating to in-laws were simply too great. Before they married, they had talked about this only a little, and he had thought that after marriage she might reconsider and be willing to go. But then, he mused, maybe she thought I would change my mind about her church too! She seemed to hope so at times, even though she seldom said much. So, we both have to give up some of our wishes, he concluded. I guess I had better start looking for a job in an American high school.

His job search took him to New Jersey, to a high school reputed to be the finest in the state. As he sat waiting to be interviewed, he wondered about the working conditions in this particular school. The secretary told him, "We've had seven music teachers in six years. This is getting ridiculous." She also said that 150 applications had come in for the job, and he would be the fiftieth one interviewed. So maybe it was a good place to work after all, Francis thought, but he still wondered about those seven previous teachers.

During the interview the superintendent studied Francis's resumé for a long time. "Hmm," he mused. "You held that church music job for quite a few years." He read on. "Ed Muskie? Is this the Senator Muskie?" Francis had included some programs with his resumé, and the senator's name appeared on one of these.

"Yes," Francis replied.

"That's impressive. I'm one of the few Democrats in town," the superintendent explained. "I know Senator Muskie. He is one of the people who can run this country."

Finally he laid down the papers and said, "Well, I'd like to hire you. Since district policies prohibit hiring someone who is not a citizen, I'll have to make a special appeal to the board of education and to the state department of education. I'll go ahead because I really want you to work here."

He started to dismiss Francis, then remembered. "Oh, by the way, I'll skip some steps on the wage scale so you won't have to start from scratch. And one more thing. I think you're the person we need. If you'll promise to stick around for a few years, I'll do everything possible to work on the legal matters."

At the first staff meeting the superintendent introduced Francis and said, "We've had a hard time with our music teachers, but now we've found a man who looks as if he's capable of handling things. He's not a citizen of the United States, but he has officially declared his intention to become one." Then the superintendent turned to Francis and shook his hand, "We welcome you," he said, while the staff applauded.

Until their move to New Jersey, Francis and Nancy had both attended their own churches each week. Now, however, Francis's attendance dwindled. His new job kept him quite busy, he reasoned with himself. Besides, after all his involvement with the music of the church, it seemed nice to take a break.

One morning a few months after their move Francis heard Nancy in the kitchen. He looked at his watch, then at the calendar. What was she doing at home at ten o'clock on Saturday morning? he wondered. Usually Nancy took Yumi, the new baby, and went to the Adventist church.

He went to the kitchen. "Aren't you and Yumi going to church today?"

Nancy looked sheepish and replied, "No."

Francis waited. He was curious about this and wanted an explanation, but he didn't want to say something wrong.

Nancy continued, "I guess the last time I went I got discouraged. I didn't feel as if I belonged. And Yumi was so fussy, and they had no mother's room. The speaker was so negative. The regular preacher was gone, and a lay preacher gave the sermon. He convinced me of what a sinner I am—it was such negative psychology!" She made a face, then grinned. "Another thing. I don't like leaving you in the mornings either. You have to go away early every day of the week, and I feel guilty about leaving you on the morning when we can be together."

Francis grinned back at her. So Saturday might eventually become a normal day after all! That day he noticed Nancy didn't do any extra work, as usual, but as the weeks slipped by he observed that she began to cook more, and finally he spotted her doing the laundry on Saturday. He didn't care. He began to enjoy Saturday at home.

After about a year in New Jersey. Francis's interest in the Catholic Church revived. He had found an exciting church, located in the mountains about a half-hour's drive away. Here he attended a weekly service called the "dialogue sermon." After the priest preached, he invited the people to ask questions or make comments. Francis liked this kind of discussion, and he tried to get Nancy to attend also.

"This church really cares about people," he told her. "They have a fund to help poor or needy individuals."

"Really?" Nancy sounded mildly interested.

"It's becoming a very popular place too," Francis continued. "People are even bussed in from towns as far as fifty miles away. After the service we go into the social hall and have coffee and doughnuts and talk for a while. It's a really nice atmosphere. And they study the Bible a lot!"

"Sounds different," Nancy conceded.

They attended a few of the Sunday services, and then Francis wanted to know what Nancy thought about this particular Catholic church.

"It's fine," she told him. "but—" she hesitated.

"But what?"

"But it feels foreign. It's a pleasant enough place, and the people seem to care, but I don't feel like I really belong."

Francis continued to attend this church, and Nancy sometimes accompanied him. Once or twice that summer they also went to an Adventist church, a different one this time. But Francis could sense the tension. He realized neither he nor Nancy intended to make a change in religion. That part of their lives loomed as a threat to a peaceful relationship. Of course, he couldn't see why he should make any change at all. Nancy had been satisfied with the fact that he lived a good Christian life. And he didn't really care that she felt some kinship with Adventists. She didn't talk about her religion very much anymore.

Nancy still taught some violin lessons at home, even though they now had three children, and, because of this, she got acquainted with a well-to-do, educated, and influential family, the Churchills. All the children came to take lessons, and sometimes after the lessons Nancy and Mrs. Churchill would chat.

"I had an interesting conversation with Mrs. Churchill today," Nancy said to Francis one evening. "She told me about an exciting spiritual experience they've had."

"What was that?"

"Well, she said that their guardian angels revealed themselves and changed their lives."

"What?" Francis sounded incredulous. "How did they do that?"

"She told me the messages come through automatic handwriting. You put a pen or pencil into your hand, and your hand will move automatically as the spirit impresses you."

Francis thought about that. Back in Japan he had

watched Shinto priests as they prayed to cast out evil spirits. As a Catholic he believed that priests had the power to exorcise evil spirits. This, however, was something new. He had never heard of this kind of communication with the spirit world. "I don't like it," he told Nancy. "And I don't think you should have anything to do with it either."

"Perhaps not," Nancy agreed. "It does sound peculiar, doesn't it?"

Francis soon forgot about the evening, and Nancy didn't mention it again. But eventually Francis became conscious of a strange feeling when at home. He couldn't point out what caused this; but he sensed it for about a week, and it made him uneasy. On one particular night he felt shaky and nervous and wondered why. A strong impulse directed him to go to the dining-room doors and open them. As he did so, it seemed that an inner voice said, "Go to the music stand. You will find a note." He followed this direction and crossed the room to the music stand. He rifled through the music and other papers and soon found a note. He looked at it carefully and then took it to Nancy.

"What's this?" he confronted her.

Nancy took the note. She didn't argue or make excuses. She simply said, "I've been to several meetings with the Churchills, and I've learned more about their type of religion."

Francis's anger flared. He tore the note and flung it to the floor. "You've got to give up this thing, or—"

"I've been looking for something spiritual," Nancy defended herself.

"I'm going to get the priest to rid us of this spirit," Francis shouted. "I can feel it in this house." Then he thought about their three children, Paul just a year old now. "I don't want any of this to affect our children."

"I really don't like your calling a priest," Nancy protested. "It seems silly."

"Either you go through with a session with the priest, or we're going to split." Francis had never felt so upset before, or so scared. He couldn't explain why this incident upset him so, but neither was he in a mood to analyze it. He slammed his fist on the table and shouted, "I can't live this way, and I don't want a spirit hurting our family."

Nancy looked astonished and just a little scared herself. They stared at each other, and finally Nancy relented. "If it makes you happy, go ahead."

Francis contacted the priest from the church in the mountains. He came, took out his container of holy water, and sprinkled some in every room. Francis thought he seemed quite casual about it, but felt better when the priest wanted to pray. Then he instructed them to call the name of Jesus and to hold a crucifix whenever the spirit troubled their home again.

Several days later a friend from the Adventist church happened to give Nancy a book. *Ellen White: Prophet of Destiny*, Nancy read from the cover. Immediately her interest arose. At the same time she continued to read books by Edgar Cayce, the "sleeping prophet." Accounts of his visions, spoken while in a trance, intrigued her.

Francis didn't pay much attention to her reading until Nancy spoke to him about it one night.

"I walked into the kitchen today," she related, "and on the table I spotted the book about Ellen White that I've been reading. On the kitchen counter I saw the books by Edgar Cayce. Then a very strange feeling came over me."

Francis sat up, interested. He knew little about Edgar Cayce, except that most people labeled him a spiritualist, and he knew even less about Ellen White. "So, what was the feeling?"

"I thought to myself, 'I have to make a choice. Do I keep reading Ellen White, or do I believe in Edgar Cayce?'" Nancy paused. "I really felt that I had come to a decision point."

"What did you decide? What did you do?"

"Suddenly I had the answer. I knew what to do. I picked up the Edgar Cayce books and walked over to the wood stove. Then I threw them in there and shut the door."

After this Nancy and Francis felt they should study about religion more, and this time do it together. "Nancy," Francis asked. "would you agree if a priest came to teach us the catechism?" When she hesitated he quickly added, "This way we could make sure the bad spirit will leave us alone."

Nancy agreed. "All right. I'm curious about the Catholic beliefs." Then she got a gleam in her eye. "And if we study, we'll find out what the real truth is, won't we?"

When the priest came, he brought with him a large book. "Now this book will teach you the history of the church," he said to Nancy. "You will learn about the symbolism and the signs."

Nancy flipped through the 600-page volume. "But what about your doctrines? Can you defend them with the Bible?" She looked sharply at the priest.

"The Catholic Church is full of tradition, and this book will tell you everything you need to know about the church."

Nancy didn't seem convinced, but argued no more and the priest left.

Several weeks went by, and once each week the priest visited Nancy and Francis. Nancy never seemed to run out of questions, and each question seemed to precipitate an argument. Francis got worried. He hadn't realized how well Nancy knew the Bible. And watching the priest back off and become reluctant to discuss anything alarmed him. Finally the priest stopped coming. Francis called him the next day. "Father, what's happening? I need your help. I wish you'd continue your visits and help me out. I don't know where to go from here."

"I don't think I can do anything with your wife. She's so stubborn." The priest sounded annoyed.

"But she's searching for what is really right," Francis protested.

"She already knows what she believes," the priest replied. "She's not going to open up her mind to anything different."

"But people from her church are visiting us too," Francis argued. "They study with us. I need you to balance them off," he pleaded.

But the priest refused. Discouraged, Francis hung up the phone.

The weekly visits from Lou, the Seventh-day Adventist, continued. Francis didn't know who had arranged for his first visit. Nancy said she hadn't called anyone. Maybe they simply noticed that Nancy seldom attended church.

Each Tuesday night Lou came over. Once he told Francis, "I'm an ex-Catholic." Francis thought, You're not going to change my religion. But he couldn't help admiring the man. He knew that Lou had given up a well-paying position in a social security office just to teach people about the Bible. And Francis marveled at his patience.

Lou took Nancy and Francis through the book of Hebrews, then through Romans. All the time Francis thought, It sounds like a foreign language. Of course he could pronounce the words as he read the Bible texts, but the meaning escaped him.

It wouldn't have surprised him if Lou had turned to him and said something like, "You dumb Japanese," but he didn't. He just allowed Francis to argue, and he kept answering him with Bible texts. Sometimes when topics like Sabbath keeping or righteousness by faith came up, Francis would get very hostile. Then Lou simply said, "Now don't get upset. I'll leave you alone." But he always returned the following week.

As the weeks went by the turmoil inside Francis increased. When the church in the mountains announced a special spiritual retreat, Francis welcomed the news. Whenever he attended this kind of retreat he had always received a special blessing.

When he entered the church for the first evening meeting he paused at the door. An uneasy, strange feeling was creeping over him. He couldn't understand this new feeling. Shaking his head, he tried to ignore it.

Inside, he could only find a seat by walking down to the very front. Just as he sat down, a young woman with a guitar stood up and began to sing contemporary spiritual songs. That sounded vaguely familiar. He remembered when the Catholic Church began to allow a folk mass for young people. He had become involved with a group of musicians who began to write and arrange music for the new type of mass. He himself had written some of the music. Now he saw how those beginnings of the folk mass had spread and reached this church in the mountains of New Jersey. He shifted uneasily in his seat and glanced at the people in the row behind him. He noticed that some of the women's eyes looked extremely bright and glittery. That disturbed him, but he couldn't help looking at one woman in particular. He thought how much her eyes glowed like an animal's in the dark.

Then his attention was drawn to the front again. The priest introduced a couple who began to speak. Francis heard them say, "The Holy Spirit has done so much for our lives." Next they related one incident after another. Then the songs began again and after that more testimonies.

Finally the guest speaker, a visiting priest, was introduced. After the preliminary greetings to his audience, he said, "I have come here to deliver my message about the charismatic movement."

So that was it! Francis had heard about groups of Catholics who claimed they had the "gifts of the Spirit" which enabled them to speak in tongues and lay their hands on the sick to heal them.

"Tonight you will be rebaptized by the Holy Spirit," the speaker continued.

That made no sense to Francis. He knew that Catholics believed in only one baptism—once baptized, baptized forever.

"The Holy Spirit has been missing in your lives," the speaker intoned, warming to his message.

Francis began to feel nervous. He looked around uneasily to see if he could sneak away. If he tried to leave now, he would disturb the tightly packed audience. He noticed that all eyes seemed focused on the speaker. This is just like a scary movie, he thought to himself. He wondered if the service would ever end!

When it finally did, Francis spoke to no one. He waded through the crowd against the current surging forward to meet the speaker. Once outside, Francis breathed deeply. Never had he felt the walls close in on him like that. "I'm never going back in there," he vowed and headed into the night.

Chapter Nine

"But I don't want to go to camp meeting," Francis protested.

Nancy's eyes pleaded, but she said nothing.

"I didn't like the church services either," Francis reminded her.

"Yes, I know," Nancy spoke. "Neither one of us liked them, but since I have found a different Adventist church and a new minister has been appointed, you have enjoyed going with me once in a while."

Francis grunted in reluctant agreement. He had to admit to himself that going to the Seventh-day Adventist church wasn't so bad anymore. The new minister, young Pastor Mike, had something good to say, and he didn't take forever to say it either. Besides, he liked the young preacher's positive attitude. Increasingly they stayed for the Sabbath dinner potluck, and Francis discovered that vegetarian meals could be quite tasty after all. The church certainly had good cooks!

But he still didn't like the loud Amens when the audience agreed with the preacher. And he still couldn't get used to some of the doctrines. Righteousness by faith especially bothered him. He had been taught that if a person worked hard enough, he would go to heaven. It didn't seem fair that being a good citizen and doing good things for the community as well as for God wouldn't get him to heaven—but believing in Christ would. And when Lou had brought up the idea of the "state of the dead," as he called it, Francis really felt bothered. He remembered kneeling with his grandmother in front of the Shinto shrine in their home, the shrine that listed their ancestors. And he remembered the ancestor worship in the Buddhist temple. No, lots of things he couldn't agree with, and now he didn't want to be exposed to any more at this camp meeting.

Suddenly he realized Nancy still sat there, looking at him expectantly and waiting for him to say something.

"Oh, all right," he moaned. Some time out in the country wouldn't hurt, he thought. He didn't have to listen if he didn't want to.

When they drove onto the campgrounds, Nancy and Francis found a place had already been reserved for them, right next to Lou and his family. That evening, as the two families ate their meal together, Lou said, "Francis, I'll wake you up at 5:30 tomorrow morning so that we can go to the six o'clock meeting together."

Francis didn't mind getting up early. After all, at the seminary he always attended the 5:30 morning worship. The idea of an early-morning meeting seemed both familiar and refreshing.

The next morning he and Lou walked around the lake and entered the tent. Francis settled back in his chair to listen to the speaker, a Dr. Coffman from a university in Michigan, but as soon as the man began to speak Francis leaned forward with interest. Righteousness by faith! That topic again!

He listened carefully, and every morning came back to listen some more. By Wednesday morning Francis began to say to himself, "Yes, that's right!" That particular morning Dr. Coffman asked the audience to separate into small groups and pray together. Lou and his wife formed a group with Francis and began to pray. While they prayed Francis felt impressed that he had finally found the truth—the right message. Tears came to his eyes. I know it's right, he kept thinking.

On the way back to the tent he wondered, How can I accept all those ideas? If I do, I can't continue my work. He felt he must get away to consider all possible angles. Maybe from a distance he could gain a clearer understanding of what he had experienced that day and what he should do about it.

"Nancy, I'm going home to check on the house and the dog," he said when he stepped into the tent.

"All right," Nancy agreed. "While you're home you can pick up some groceries. Here's a list."

All the way home Francis argued with himself: I can't do this; I can't join this church. But I know it's right. I've studied all this for a year now, and I know it's right. But I can't do this!

That night he couldn't sleep. He prayed and meditated and paced the floor. When the morning sun flooded his room, he felt better. I know this is absolutely right, he said to himself. I can't argue with it any more.

But when the call came to be baptized and join the church, Francis demurred. His good, high-paying job was at stake. His marching band had been a smashing success. He had worked hard with it, and he liked the students too. Now he also had excellent community backing. He just didn't want to give all that up. Besides, he had already signed a contract. No, he decided, he wasn't ready for that—not yet.

The football games started. On Saturday morning Francis dropped off his family at church and headed for the football field. Already raindrops hit the windshield, and by the time he got to the high school the rain was coming down in sheets. Francis called the football coach. "Are we going to cancel the game?"

"No," the coach said.

"But the uniforms and boots will get all messed up," Francis complained, "and the sheet music will get wet."

"It's the opening game, and we have to play," the coach answered. "We've got to win this one. We've got to better the record from last season," the coach argued.

Francis understood—a new coach, a new season, and a popular band director. Of course they had to go through with it.

During the half-time show Francis wondered if they had all lost their senses. Rain dripped down his collar, and his shoes sloshed and squished in the mud. He gritted his teeth and led the band out on the field.

The team won, but Francis thought only about having to get the uniforms cleaned, the wet music dried out, and some damp pads replaced on the clarinets.

On Friday night of the next week dark clouds rolled over the New Jersey countryside, and rain pelted the town with a vengeance. On Saturday morning the band went through the half-time show half-heartedly, bucking the driving wind and rain. As soon as the show ended the band disappeared into the building as if a magic wand had been waved.

By the third rainy Saturday people began to say, "What's going on? This certainly is strange weather!"

Francis began to wonder, too, as he and the band stood in the sidelines watching their team play. This day's game was important. Their team had never defeated this particular visiting team. By the end of the game everyone cheered, as much for the chance to get out of the rain as for the victory.

By the fourth week, when he got home on Saturday afternoon, Francis said to Nancy, "What's going on? I'm soaking wet, the kids are getting colds, the instruments are getting ruined, and we keep leaving shoes in the mud."

"Well," Nancy answered, "one of the church members suggested that we all pray for you because the members want to see you in church."

"So," Francis wondered, "what does that have to do with all this rain?"

"They asked God to do something about your not coming," Nancy explained.

"Oh, sure," Francis exclaimed. "I don't believe in that kind of stuff."

But when it rained the following weekend also, Francis was no longer quite so certain. At home that day after the game he said to Nancy, "Who's the woman who suggested the idea of praying for me?"

Nancy told him. He immediately went to the phone.

"Ma'am," he said, "I understand you have been praying for me. But all this rain isn't doing anyone any good."

"Yes," she said, "we did pray because we want to help you. We want to see you in church."

"But the rain," Francis protested. "It doesn't stop the games anyway. Now would you please pray for nice weather?"

"OK," she agreed.

Fifteen minutes later the sky began to clear. Francis went back to the phone and called her again. "It's clearing! The sky is brightening!"

"Yes," she answered. "I see that too. I guess God is listening to us."

"Just coincidence," Francis said.

"Maybe." The woman laughed and Francis laughed with her.

But the Saturdays after that were clear and sunny. A coincidence? Francis just didn't know.

A month later Mike, the church pastor, called. "Francis, we need your help with the Five-Day Plan to Stop Smoking sessions."

"Sure," Francis answered. "What do you want me to do?" He wondered whether the pastor knew of his fondness for smoking pipes.

"Oh, there are lots of jobs. Come next Sunday night, and we'll put you to work."

Sunday night arrived and Francis shivered as he got out of his car at the church. A cold front had come through, and the temperature hovered menacingly low. Then it began to snow. This presented him with a chance to avoid going inside right way. Francis offered to direct the parking. He didn't want to go inside. How could he, a smoker, go to help a group trying to stop smoking?

About fifteen minutes later someone came out and said, "Hey, we need you inside. One of the leaders didn't show up."

"Not me," Francis protested. "I can't do that kind of thing. I would rather stay out here."

"But we don't have anyone else. We really need you."

"All right," Francis groaned. "I'll do it."

He went in and sat in the last row. Six men and women, all middle aged, also sat there. He felt awkward and thought he ought to say something, so he leaned over and greeted them, "Hi! I'm Francis." He couldn't bring himself to say, "I'm the leader of this group." Finally the meeting ended.

On the second night Francis hoped the missing

group leader would show up, but instead Francis had to meet with his group again.

During the day he called each of the six people. His instructions were to encourage them in their struggle to quit. "Have you had a good day?" he asked. "Did you cut down or throw out a pack of cigarettes? Keep it up!" As he made these calls twice a day, he felt like a hypocrite. Often he clutched his pipe and smoked while dialing the numbers.

Nancy watched him for several days, then inquired, "How can you do that?"

"What?" Francis pretended not to understand.

"Talk to people about smoking while you are smoking yourself."

"I don't know," Francis confessed. "But these people *want* to stop. I don't. I enjoy it too much."

On Wednesday night the audience at the stop-smoking clinic watched a film. That film caught Francis's attention with descriptions of lung diseases, effects of smoking on nonsmokers, and possibility of cancer. It scared Francis. He thought of his children. Did his habit really affect others?

When he got home that night he didn't go in right away but paced back and forth in the driveway, smoking all the time. Maybe if I don't smoke inside the house it would be OK, he rationalized. Then he stopped. What about the effect on me? he wondered. Shouldn't I care about that? Finally he declared to the silent night—"I quit!"

The next day when he made his usual calls to the group members he said, "I have something to confess. I've been smoking until last night, so I know what you're going through. Stick with it, and we'll beat this thing together." That night he confessed to the entire group, "I've been a hypocrite, but now I've put away my pipe and tobacco. I encourage all of you to quit like I have."

For two weeks following the stop-smoking clinic Francis didn't touch his pipe, but every time he walked into his study he spotted it. How it tempted him—a beautiful, expensive wood pipe. He opened the can of tobacco and sniffed. What aroma! He had to drive clear to Pennsylvania to buy this special brand.

Nancy passed by the door and stopped. "Why don't you just throw that thing away?" she inquired.

Francis picked up the pipe and stroked the beautiful wood grain. "How can I do that? I'd rather send it to my father."

"What good would that do? I know you want your father to stop smoking too. Why tempt him?"

Francis thought about that and realized everything finally made sense. He looked at his pipe once more, then gathered up all his smoking things. "Away it all goes!" he declared.

"Then do it now and do it fast," Nancy said, "before you start caressing your pipe again!"

On the morning of the last game of the football season Francis got up at 4:30. Secluding himself in his study, he drafted a letter. After he checked it and retyped it, he folded it and put it in an envelope. Then he went to the special Thanksgiving Day game.

His team won, and his band marched through town. "We'd rather come see your half-time show," parents said, "than the football game." They presented him with a banner that the band members proudly displayed—"WADA BAND."

A few days later Francis got a call from the high school. "The superintendent wants to see you right away," the secretary announced. "He doesn't care what classes you have. You just come right away."

The superintendent greeted Francis with a smile and said, "I read your letter, but I don't quite understand what you are trying to say, so I want you to explain. Of course, I cannot accept your resignation."

Francis sat down and told the superintendent about how he had studied the Bible for a year now and had learned about the Sabbath.

"But what's the difference between Sunday worship and Saturday worship?"

Francis explained to the best of his ability and concluded, "I believe I have to keep all the commandments of God, including the fourth."

"Well, can't you at least work during the football season and the rest of the time we won't ask you to do any Saturday work?"

"No. That would not be possible."

"But can't you ask your church officials for an OK just for the football season?"

"No," Francis said again. "I won't ask them because it's really just between God and me and has nothing to do with the church officials."

"Well, I guess you're right about that," the superintendent reflected. He thought for a few minutes. "Well, what if I get you another assistant?"

That impressed Francis. He already had two assistants, and that in a school of only 650 students.

The superintendent misinterpreted Francis's silence, "I'll get you another assistant, and you don't need to go to the football games. Just train the students and the assistant will direct on Saturdays."

Francis answered. "That's not my way of handling things. If I'm involved I want to do the work from beginning to end. It would be poor for student morale."

"Well, maybe if I offer you a raise?"

"Money has nothing to do with it," Francis insisted.

"I'll give you a raise that will take you to $30,000." The superintendent just couldn't understand.

"No," Francis repeated. "It isn't the money. For that matter, I don't know what I'll do after this school year, but I'm not resigning because of money."

"Well, then I will have to accept your resignation?" the superintendent sounded incredulous.

"Well, now that the football season is over, I'll finish this school year. Then I will look for another job."

That Christmas Eve Francis and Nancy were both baptized. After the service, as they drove home, Nancy broke the comfortable silence. "What a beautiful night!" She peered out of the car window toward the sky. The clear winter sky shone with stars, and only thin wisps of clouds scurried across the moon as the cold winter wind urged them on.

Then she turned her gaze back to the dark road ahead and said softly, "I know that in Japanese tradition, only the weak need religion, but I think you're a strong man, because you studied something for yourself and stood firm in your convictions."

Francis grunted, the only response he could think of to this compliment. He mused on how God had led in his life by using people such as Lou, circumstances like rainy days, encounters with spiritualism, and the Catholic church to cause him to study the Bible for himself.

Nancy broke into his thoughts. "I'm happy, and yet I have regrets too." She sounded a little sad.

Francis turned in surprise. "Why?"

"I could have been a strong influence on the Churchills. By compromising my convictions I brought heartache to both of us. And I hope some of our disagreements over religion haven't hurt the children."

Francis interrupted her, "Don't blame yourself!

What matters is that the Lord was patient with us, and now we are both content because of His mercy. It really doesn't pay to talk about what we should have done long ago!"

Nancy smiled and they drove the rest of the way home in silence. Christmas lights on houses and trees twinkled merrily at the close of this special Christmas Eve.

After church the next Sabbath Lou met Francis at the door and asked, "What will you do next year?"

Francis could only say, "I don't know."

Lou smiled. "God will lead you to the right place of work. You are such a successful teacher. Why don't you work for the denomination?"

That spring Francis received his copy of the teacher evaluation form. The superintendent had written: "As always, Mr. Wada has done an outstanding job in each of the areas in which he has worked. Anyone who has witnessed the amazing reformation of the high school marching band can attest to the singular ability and effectiveness of Mr. Wada. Realizing that Mr. Wada has submitted his resignation I wish only to point out the very fine work he has done over the past six years. Mr. Wada is truly a remarkable person and will be sorely missed."

Francis smiled at this. It felt good to be praised, but now what?

Lou had an idea. "Just sending out applications won't do a lot of good. Why don't you go to the General Conference and talk to someone there?"

The idea scared Francis, but finally he got the courage to make an appointment.

In spite of Francis's fears the meeting went well. Dr. Millett interviewed him and said, "Your recommendations are superb. I am impressed by you, and I'll do something out of the ordinary. I'll write a letter to all principals of Seventh-day Adventist academies and to the superintendents too." Francis appreciated that, but what impressed him more was Dr. Millett's suggestion, "Let's pray to God that some suitable work will open for you."

Three days after the meeting Francis received a copy of Dr. Millett's letter: "Brother Wada has very high recommendations and is a gifted musician. He has offered his talents to the church. He has been exceptionally successful in teaching high school music in the wealthiest school in New Jersey, but Sabbath problems now confront him." In closing the letter said, "We trust the Lord will direct him into an appropriate place in His service."

That same evening a long-distance call came from Nebraska. "This is the principal of Platte Valley Academy in Nebraska," the voice on the other end of the line said.

Where, thought Francis frantically, is Nebraska?

"I received the letter about you from Dr. Millett today," the principal continued.

Francis hoped to make an appropriate comment, but had to ask, "Where is Nebraska?"

"It's in the Midwest."

"Is it cold there?"

"Well, yes," the principal answered. "But it doesn't get too bad. Why?"

Francis laughed. "When Dr. Millett asked me, 'Is there any place you don't want to go,' I answered, 'I don't want to go to the northern Midwest because I hear it's really cold.' "

"Well," the principal explained, "Nebraska is in the central Midwest—not quite so cold. Why don't you visit the school? Then we can discuss the job."

Francis did fly out. After landing in Lincoln he drove the hundred miles to the academy. The openness of the fields and pastures contrasted sharply with the gently rolling hills of New Jersey. The cold wind buffeted his little rental car, and the endless sky seemed to stretch on forever. Finally he came to a sign by the roadside, and he turned down a dirt road toward a cluster of modern buildings.

After his visit to the academy, Francis and Nancy prayed earnestly, especially since they also had another job offer right in New Jersey. Finally Francis called the principal and said, "You win. We're coming."

Now they had to sell the house. For a month no one came to see the house. Finally a young couple spotted the For Sale sign and came to the door. After looking around and asking a few questions, they said, "We like the price, but this is the first house we've looked at. We'd like to look some more and then we'll come back."

The next night another young couple came. They looked around for only about ten minutes and then faced Francis. "We don't have much money, but this house is perfect for us. Would you take $50,000?"

Francis gasped. He had priced the house at $52,000, expecting to come down. The realtor had said, "You should be happy if you get $46,000."

He tried to control his excitement. "Let me call my wife. She's at the church, taking cooking classes."

In the kitchen he dialed the church number and said softly, "Someone wants to buy the house. They want to know if we'll take $50,000 for it."

"Fifty thousand!" Nancy screamed into his ear. "Of course!"

Francis grinned. More and more he marveled at how

the Lord was working things out.

As school ended, Francis and Nancy decided to go to camp meeting once more to say good-bye to their friends. As they were packing for camp meeting Francis got a phone call.

"Long distance from Japan," the operator said.

Francis listened to the message. "Your mother is very ill. She has had a stroke. She probably won't survive. Can you come?"

Chapter Ten

Immediately Francis called a travel agent. "I need an airline ticket to Tokyo," he said. "It's an emergency. How soon can you book me on a flight?"

"Sorry, sir," the agent replied. "All the airlines are on strike."

On strike! Francis had forgotten that. "Isn't there anything you can do for me?"

"Sorry, sir," the man repeated. "But leave your phone number. If any flights to Japan open up, we will be sure to call you."

For the next three days Francis frantically tried everything he could think of. He even called the secretary of state's office in Washington to see if any military planes might take him to Japan. No results.

At the end of the third day the travel agent called him. "TWA is now flying to Japan. We have you booked, but you must get to New York immediately."

"What papers do I need? A visa?"

"No, sir, you don't need one, and you can pick up an emergency passport at Kennedy Airport."

On the way to New York, Francis picked up his sister, who now lived in the United States also. After the jet took off, Francis stared out of the small window into the billowy gray clouds. Memories that hadn't entered his mind for a long time now crowded in. What would it be like to be back in Japan, to see relatives, to talk to his father again? He hoped he would see his mother alive once again.

He remembered when he and Nancy got married. His parents had not sent angry letters or called him long distance. Instead they sent gifts—a new camera for him and a kimono for Nancy. But later an uncle wrote, "Your parents are very upset. They say you are not fulfilling your duties as a son." Francis wondered how much guilt he should feel. Of course he cared about his parents, but other emotions blurred feelings of love he might have felt.

Finally the plane landed at the mammoth new airport outside of Tokyo. At the customs counter Francis's sister said, "I'll go on down and wait for our luggage, since it will probably take you a while."

Francis nodded and gave his passport to the customs official. The man studied it for a long time, longer than Francis thought necessary. Finally he looked up and spoke sternly, "You have no Japanese visa."

"My travel agent said I didn't need one," Francis explained.

"As an American citizen, you need one," the official stated flatly.

Before Francis could think of something reasonable to say, two other customs officials approached, grabbed his arms, and commanded, "Come this way."

They sat him down in an office. He stared at the half-dozen officials now glaring at him.

"Why have you entered Japan without a visa?"

Again Francis tried to explain, but they wouldn't listen.

"The first thing we should do is put you in jail," one of them said.

Francis cringed under their hostile interrogation. "My sister is waiting at the baggage claim," he told them. "My mother is dying. I'm not here to cause any trouble."

"You will have to return to the United States on the next flight and reenter properly—with a visa," the official said.

"But my mother is seriously ill, and I don't have that much money!"

"Well, then fly to Hawaii and get the proper papers."

The officials didn't seem to believe Francis, and that fact scared him. His mind flashed back to a time when he had feared he would lose a visa—now he didn't even have one to lose!

Finally he convinced them to call the hospital. One official did so, then said, "Well, you must be telling the truth. Now you need to fill out these forms for the Ministry of Interior." He handed Francis about six sheets of paper. "You might receive a special temporary pass to enter Japan. Come back tomorrow by nine in the morning. If you don't show up, you are in serious trouble."

"Nine o'clock!" Francis groaned. He looked at his watch. Six o'clock in the evening. What must his sister think! He had been in the office for over two hours. Now it would take an hour and a half to get to Tokyo and then he had to return to the airport by nine in the morning. Besides, he had to fill out all these forms.

Finally the customs officials allowed Francis to leave the office. He located his frantic sister, and together they boarded the bus for Tokyo. Francis looked out of the window, marveling how things had changed. "Why, it looks like wartime!" he exclaimed. "Look at all the military out there." Then the bus stopped at a checkpoint. All the passengers and their luggage had to be searched before the bus could continue.

"What's going on?" Francis asked at the third checkpoint.

"There's been a lot of rioting. Students have stormed the airport and vandalized it. Many people, like the farmers around here, didn't want the airport built, and students have joined in the protest."

That explained at least part of his problem. The customs officials may have thought he belonged to a radical student group! That's why they had warmed up a bit when he mentioned he had served in the Japanese army twelve years ago. If only he had remembered his old Japanese passport!

Finally they reached the hospital. Softly he tiptoed up to the bed. His mother lay unconscious. Again memories flooded over him—the times when she had been happy and active, painting or playing ball with neighbors and relatives. She had changed because of worry and hard work after the family lost its money. He sat down by her beside and wondered just how much that part of her life had contributed to her stroke.

The next morning Francis rushed back to Narita Airport. Exhausted because of the long trip from America and the sleepless night spent with his mother, he scarcely noticed the turmoil outside of the barriers surrounding the airport. At the checkpoints he smiled wearily when the guards scrutinized his passport, and finally he arrived at the customs office.

"We were able to secure a temporary visa for you," the official on duty informed him. Then he added, "You looked very suspicious last night!"

A few days later Francis decided to visit Aioi Mura. He boarded the train and eagerly watched the scenery. How much things had changed! Homes and factories crowded the rice fields. Tall buildings shut out the sun. Roads and cars cut up the countryside. Aioi Mura had changed too. He wandered through the streets, stopping to stare at houses. Finally he thought, it can't be this far. He turned back and, at last, there stood his home.

He entered the house. Father, a bottle of sake in his hand, stood inside.

"Father."

Father turned, laid down the glass he had poised to raise to his lips, and came toward Francis, "Toshimasa! How good to see you!"

Father and son sat down. They had so much to share about the last twelve years. Francis told him of life in America, and Father related what had happened to Aioi Mura since he left.

As the evening wore on, Father seemed to grow more pensive. Finally he gave Francis a searching look and asked, "Now are you ready to return home?"

Francis reacted in surprise. "No, that's not possible! My family is in America and happy there, and I have just accepted a teaching position."

Father frowned. "Are you forgetting your duty as the eldest and the only son?"

Francis didn't reply. He realized he had dishonored his parents in several ways in the past—in such ways as studying music against their wishes—and had defied Japanese traditions by not bringing home his bride. He regretted having embarrassed them, but the decisions he had made now seemed to fit into a pattern. He reflected on how the Lord had probably led him before he even knew of such guidance.

"You should be here to support us and care for us," Father said, frowning deeply as his penetrating look searched Francis's face. "You and your wife should consider your duty to us, especially now since your mother is ill."

"Father, it's not possible," Francis began.

His father's anger erupted. "You have failed us as a son! You have disgraced us once again!"

Francis watched as his father raged. Suddenly he felt like the little boy Toshimasa again—Toshimasa, waiting for his father's frequent outbursts of temper to subside; Toshimasa, watching his father storm out of the house after an argument with his mother; Toshimasa, yearning for his parents' approval but usually missing it; Toshimasa, the little boy on the railroad track. What a homecoming!

During the two days he spent in Aioi Mura he contacted some of his high school friends and teachers. All of them urged, "Francis, stay here. We can help you find good jobs, and you can make excellent money."

That seemed true. One friend, now a musician in Tokyo symphony, found a job for Francis as an interpreter. "The pay is great," he urged. "All you need to do is say Yes."

Francis had to agree about the pay. Working for the government as an interpreter would bring him twice the salary he would get as a teacher in Nebraska, and social status as well.

Another friend arranged for him to work in the same factory where he had been employed as a student, only now he would be teaching English to the employees and management.

"All you have to do is say Yes," his friends urged.

During his last night at Aioi Mura Francis paced the floor. What decisions he faced! How his feelings churned in turmoil! He had wanted to return to Japan so that he could share his new-found faith. But on the other hand, jobs like the ones his friends had arranged for him involved working six days a week. How could he give up his faith now?

He reflected on all that had happened in the past year. God certainly had been patient and good to both him and Nancy. Because of His mercy, both of them now wanted to serve Him in the best way possible. But what was the best way? Thoughts pursued each other in Francis's mind, and he gazed through the window at the dark night. Streetlights flickered through the descending fog. A dog barked. A siren screamed some blocks away and faded into the distance. The dog's bark ended in a long howl. Francis turned way from the window and walked over to the bed.

"I have to sort through all these thoughts that keep running through my head," Francis fretted as he looked at his watch. Only three more hours before daylight. He lay down on his bed, turned out the lamp, and stared toward the ceiling. The darkness enveloped him, and the hushed night seemed to wait for his decision.

Faint streaks of light broke through the cloudy sky as Francis awoke and knelt by his bed. Then once again he headed for the window. He watched Aioi Mura come to life. Memories flooded him—of those times when he and his grandmother had spent days together, when he struggled to be at the top of his class, when he spent early morning hours running errands for his mother or practicing in the dark band room. He heard his father stir downstairs. He went over to the desk, sat down, took out a sheet of paper and began to write.

Dear Nancy:

Last night was short on sleep and long on decisions and prayer. I won't take time to tell you all that I had to decide, or all that has happened since I arrived here.

That can wait until I see you in a week.

But I do want to tell you that once again I'm thankful for how the Lord led in our lives. I have lain awake, recounting to myself His many blessings. Even though it will be difficult for me to leave my parents, I know God calls me to a definite work, and I cannot ignore that. My sisters and other relatives will watch over my parents. I feel I must go where I can do the most, and where, at this moment, God wants me. I must obey God rather than the traditions of Japan. I love my parents and my country, but I love God more.

Call the principal of Platte Valley Academy and confirm our decision to go there. Tell him we'll be moved in three weeks.

Hug Yumi, Naomi, and Paul for me.

Love,

Francis.

He signed his name with a flourish and determination. Strange—he didn't even feel tired. As he sealed the envelope, voices drifted to him through the open window. A jet streaked across the rosy morning sky. The rumble of rushing traffic rose in waves. But Francis hardly heard any of it. With a bold step he crossed the floor and headed downstairs.